lonely planet
kids

SYDNEY

City Trails

Helen Greathead

 FLOAT ON...

SYDNEY IN THE DARK

THE NAME GAME

WET, WET, WET

THE CITY'S SETTLERS

GO OUTDOORS

SYDNEY SHAPES

ASIA IN OZ

SKY HIGH

LOOKING GOOD

MAKING A SPLASH

DEADLY SYDNEY

BENEATH THE SURFACE

MUNCH TIME!

**Hi...
we are Amelia
and Marco, and
we've created 19
awesome themed
trails for you
to follow.**

The pushpins on this map
mark the starting points,
and each trail is packed
with secrets, stories, and
lots of other cool stuff. So
whether you are a foodie, a
sports fanatic, or a wildlife
expert, this book has got
something for you!

CONTENTS

PAGE NUMBER

IN THE BEGINNING

The Gadigal people lived in the area now known as Sydney for thousands of years. They understood the land, its plants, and animals, and knew how to use them and look after them. Then, in 1770, the Europeans came and everything changed. However, Aboriginal traditions have survived and are thriving in the city today.

250+
The number of different language groups living in Australia in 1788.

400
The number of Aboriginal nations in Australia at the time.

START

KU-RING-GAI CHASE NATIONAL PARK

THE STENCIL EFFECT IS ACHIEVED BY MIXING RED OCHER WITH WATER AND SPRAYING IT OVER YOUR HAND — USING YOUR MOUTH!

HAND SIGNS

RED HANDS CAVE, KU-RING-GAI CHASE NATIONAL PARK

Red ocher handprints were a sign to early Sydneysiders that a cave was a safe place to stay. However, these markings are part of a rich culture that the new arrivals did not understand. They were made by Aboriginal Gadigal people, who occupied this area centuries before anyone called it Sydney. When Europeans settled here in 1788, they brought horrible new diseases, such as smallpox, which killed most of the indigenous population.

GADIGAL BOYS WENT THROUGH AN INITIATION CEREMONY THAT INVOLVED HAVING A FRONT TOOTH KNOCKED OUT. IT'S THOUGHT THE GADIGAL PEOPLE RESPECTED THE EUROPEAN GOVERNOR ARTHUR PHILLIP, WHO CAME WITH THE FIRST FLEET, BECAUSE HE HAD A MISSING FRONT TOOTH, TOO.

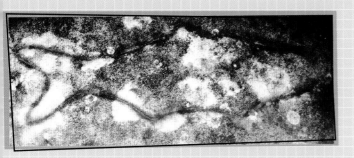

HUNDRED-YEAR-OLD SUPPER

MANLY SCENIC WALKWAY

Walkers following the coast path from Spit Bridge to Manly can spot plenty of signs of traditional Aboriginal life, from ancient drawings of boomerangs, fish, and kangaroos to old campsites and shell mounds. The Guringai people in this area collected shellfish to eat, and the piles of discarded shells are the remains of meals eaten centuries ago.

MANLY SCENIC WALKWAY

MUSEUM OF SYDNEY

SPEARING THE KANGAROO

ART GALLERY OF NEW SOUTH WALES

Drawn in the 1880s by Tommy McRae, this picture records how Aboriginal Australians hunted kangaroos. They were skilled hunters. By moving quietly downwind from their target, and with just a handheld bush for camouflage and a wooden spear, they would track and catch unsuspecting kangaroos.

ART GALLERY OF NEW SOUTH WALES

ANCIENT HISTREE

EDGE OF THE TREES, MUSEUM OF SYDNEY

These 29 huge "tree" pillars, created by artists Fiona Foley and Janet Laurence, represent the site where the Gadigal people first spotted Europeans. Each sculpture is named after one of the Aboriginal clans. Eerie voices call out as visitors walk through the columns; windows contain bone, shell, ash, and even human hair as a reminder of the people who once lived here.

ABORIGINAL ART

ALL OVER THE CITY

Aboriginal culture is the oldest continuous culture in the world. Many Aboriginal paintings are based on creation stories that date back 50,000 years. These stories are passed down through families, and in many desert areas, they are explained by drawing symbols in the sand. But some of the symbols are private and sacred, so in order to hide their meaning from outsiders, artists often cover them with dots. Many Aboriginal paintings today feature bold colors and intricate patterns created with dots.

ALL OVER THE CITY

BANGARRA DANCE THEATRE

DIARY-INSPIRED DANCE

BANGARRA DANCE THEATRE

In 2014, to celebrate its 25th anniversary, the Bangarra Dance Theatre dramatized the story of Patyegarang, an Aboriginal woman who made friends with the English Captain Dawes of the First Fleet. Dawes was interested in the local culture, so Patyegarang taught him her language. The story only came to light when Dawes' diaries were discovered nearly 200 years later – along with his translations!

BANGARRA BASES ITS DANCES ON TRADITIONAL CULTURE DATING BACK OVER 40,000 YEARS!

WHALE BAY

BOTANY BAY, LA PEROUSE

Aboriginal residents call this area Guriwal, meaning "whale," but it's also known as "La Perouse" after French explorer Jean-François de Galaup, comte de La Pérouse. A few days after the English First Fleet left, he anchored here for six weeks before sailing off... never to be seen again. Today, guided tours include the bush and beach, covering ancient stories and ways of living.

LA PEROUSE

JIBBON HEAD ABORIGINAL ENGRAVINGS SITE

search: **FIRST FLEET**

1788
The year the First Fleet sailed into Botany Bay.

11
The number of ships in the fleet.

756
The number of convicts on the ships.

7 MONTHS
The time it took the fleet to sail from England to Australia.

23
The number of convicts who died on the voyage.

THE LAW OF THE TONGUE

JIBBON HEAD ABORIGINAL ENGRAVINGS SITE

This sandstone engraving of an orca, or killer whale, is over 1,000 years old. Dharawal people had a special relationship with orcas. These creatures would help them by chasing a humpback whale until it became stranded on the sand – providing meat for a feast. The Dharawal always said thank you by throwing the humpback's tongue to the orcas. They call this "the law of the tongue." If visiting Jibbon Head, keep to the viewing platform to protect the rock engravings.

BENEATH THE SURFACE

Fascinating as it is aboveground, this trail shows that some of the city's best stories are hidden underground, or even underwater.

UNDERWATER SCOOTERS
GORDON'S BAY

Underwater scooters take snorkeling to a whole new level. Riders grip handles and press a trigger to set a propeller spinning so they can dive down and scoot through the ocean. Here, under the water, they'll buzz past starfish, cuttlefish, and anemones. They may even spot a big blue groper fish.

> BLUE GROPERS GROW UP TO 3.9 FT. (1.2 M) LONG. ALL BLUE GROPERS ARE BORN BROWN AND FEMALE. THE TRUE BLUES CHANGE COLOR, AND SEX, AS THEY GET OLDER.

START

GORDON'S BAY

WAVERLEY CEMETERY

A GRAVE EMERGENCY
WAVERLEY CEMETERY

Until June 2016, the remains of famous poets, actors, sports people, politicians, millionaires, criminals, and 200 war casualties rested peacefully in this clifftop cemetery. But that peace was shattered when violent storms caused a landslide, leaving many graves dangerously close to the cliff edge. Families of the dead were assured their loved ones would not be disturbed during repairs.

86,000
BODIES ARE BURIED HERE

1 MILLION
PEOPLE VISIT EACH YEAR

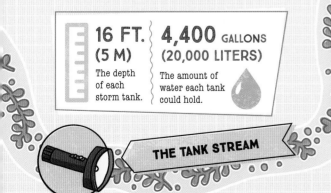

STINKING STREAM

THE TANK STREAM

In 1788, this stream flowed from an area of swampland, over several waterfalls, and into Sydney Harbour. Captain Phillip knew right away that he'd found the fresh water he needed to build a settlement. With rains sometimes torrential and sometimes nonexistent, he built storm tanks to store excess water. Phillip understood the importance of keeping the water clean, but his successors were not so careful. By 1826, the freshwater stream was a stinking sewer. As the city grew above it, the stream was covered up and forgotten.

16 FT. (5 M)
The depth of each storm tank.

4,400 GALLONS (20,000 LITERS)
The amount of water each tank could hold.

THE TANK STREAM

BOMBPROOF

ST. JAMES STATION TUNNELS

In the 1930s, grand plans to expand Sydney's underground railway were shelved because of the Great Depression. With money too tight, two completed platforms and tunnels beneath St. James station never opened. During World War II, the tunnels were used as air-raid shelters; the walls are so thick it's still impossible to pull them down. Most Sydneysiders won't ever get down here, but the tunnels are still used occasionally – some scenes in the movie *The Matrix Revolutions* were filmed here.

IN ONE OF THE TUNNELS, WATER SEEPING IN THROUGH CRACKS HAS FORMED A LAKE THAT SPANS 0.62 MILES (1 KM) AND WHICH IS 16 FT. (5 M) DEEP IN PLACES!

UNDERWATER SHOTS

SYDNEY HARBOUR

There's a wider range of sea life here than in any other harbor in the world, with undersea gardens and kelp forests, too. In 2014, Google Maps began experimenting in these waters using special cameras – with the idea of creating a "Seaview" that works just like "Street View." Divers carried the 360-degree cameras on underwater scooters and operated them via a tablet, taking around 1,000 panoramic shots per dive. They had to be careful, though – electric impulses from the scooters are thought to attract sharks!

THIS LITTLE CREATURE HIDES IN DARK HOLES ON THE HARBOR BED. IT'S CALLED A "DUBIOUS FROGFISH" BECAUSE, WHEN FISHERMEN PULL IT OUT OF THE WATER, IT REALLY DOES CROAK LIKE A FROG!

586
The number of fish species living in Sydney Harbour.

DARLING HARBOUR

SYDNEY HARBOUR

CONCRETE REEF

DARLING HARBOUR

Right by the Australian National Maritime Museum, 6.6 ft. (2 m) below the water, new reefs are growing. Six concrete balls were "planted" by museum divers in 2015. Each one had several holes and contained a special ingredient that encourages sea life to settle in and around it. The reef balls themselves don't look that special but they should be teeming with marine life before too long.

1,322 LB.
(600 KG)
The weight of each concrete mini-reef.

MAN OVERBOARD

SOUTH HEAD

On a dark and stormy night in August 1857, passenger ship SS *Dunbar* turned too sharply as it entered Sydney Harbour, lurched sideways, and careered into rocks at the foot of South Head cliffs. As the ship crashed, crew member James Johnson was flung onto the cliff face, where he stayed, clinging on desperately, until he was rescued two days later. The 63 passengers and 58 crew went down with the ship. James was the sole survivor.

SOUTH HEAD

search: HARBOR WRECKS

100+

The number of ships that lie wrecked at the bottom of Sydney Harbour. They include convict ships, passenger ferries, coal carriers, and even a Japanese submarine.

MANLY SEA LIFE SANCTUARY

UNDERWATER... WITH SHARKS!

MANLY SEA LIFE SANCTUARY

The transparent walls in Manly's "Shark Harbour" tank make visitors feel like they're underwater, as colorful fish, stingrays, turtles, and even sharks swim overhead. Manly goes one step further, though, and lets its visitors put on scuba gear and enter the tank – with actual sharks! But there's no need to panic, as these gray nurse sharks are not interested in humans. Nicknamed "Labradors of the Sea," their favorite dish is fish.

MURDOCH, ONE OF MANLY'S YOUNGEST NURSE SHARKS, WAS BORN AT THE SANCTUARY, WHICH DOESN'T COLLECT ANIMALS FROM THE WILD. BREEDING AND GETTING TO KNOW THE CREATURES IN THE TANKS MAKES IT EASIER TO HELP AND PROTECT FREE-ROAMING SHARKS.

ONCE FEARED AS MAN-EATERS, GRAY NURSE SHARKS ARE NOW PROTECTED ALL OVER AUSTRALIA.

SKY HIGH

The Sydney sky is constantly changing, with magnificent sunrises, stunning sunsets, and a dazzling display of stars at night. This trail shows a few ways the sky has influenced the city, and some good places to view it from.

"Time for lunch!"

IT'S IN THE STARS

SYDNEY OBSERVATORY

Observatory Hill is the highest point overlooking Sydney, which is why the observatory was built here in the 19th century. Back then, it was an astronomer's job to tell the time from the stars. At 1:00 p.m. each day, they would drop the time ball on the top of the observatory tower, a cannon would fire, and everyone would know the time. The observatory closed in 1982 but is now a museum.

START

SYDNEY OBSERVATORY

SYDNEY TOWER

"Race you to the top!"

HOW HIGH?

SYDNEY TOWER

Through the observation deck windows at the top of Sydney Tower, visitors get spectacular 360-degree views of the city – to the Blue Mountains on one side and the Pacific Ocean on the other. Up here, ships can be seen up to 34 miles (55 km) away! A further 52 ft. (16 m) up is the Skywalk. Brave visitors, harnessed to the building and wearing special safety suits, step onto its outdoor platform to look out across the city, and down – through the glass floor – to the ground 879 ft. (268 m) below. Yikes!

search: SYDNEY TOWER

📍 THE TURRET

The eight-story turret, or "Golden Basket," near the top of Sydney Tower has an observation deck, two restaurants, and a café.

THE GREAT EMU IN THE SKY

KU-RING-GAI CHASE NATIONAL PARK

Indigenous Australians pass on their knowledge through storytelling, sometimes using pictures in the stars. There are many stories about the "Coalsack" – a cloud of gas and dust in outer space – but the most famous tells of a great emu. A rock engraving at Ku-ring-gai Chase National Park depicts the Emu in the Sky. When the engraved emu lined up with the Emu in the Sky, it was time to collect emu eggs.

WHEN THE FIRST FLEET ANCHORED IN 1788, THE TWINKLING MILKY WAY WOULD HAVE BEEN VISIBLE TO THE NAKED EYE. TODAY, LIGHT POLLUTION MEANS YOU NEED TO USE A TELESCOPE.

KU-RING-GAI CHASE NATIONAL PARK

LUNA PARK

TO KEEP HIM LOOKING FRESH-FACED, LUNA PARK'S GIANT SMILING CLOWN HAS HAD EIGHT MAKEOVERS SINCE 1935.

UP, UP, AND AWAY

LUNA PARK

This park is nearly as old as the Sydney Harbour Bridge, and it's been entertaining the crowds since 1935. Visitors enter through the giant face of a laughing clown to experience some old-world entertainment. The park is built right on the harborside, but views of the water and the bridge are at their best 131 ft. (40 m) up at the top of the Ferris wheel.

SKY SAFARI

TARONGA ZOO

Passengers feel like they're flying in this cable car that takes them up to the entrance of the zoo. There's the amazing panorama of the Sydney skyline when they look behind them, and a bird's-eye view of the zoo when they look ahead.

TARONGA ZOO

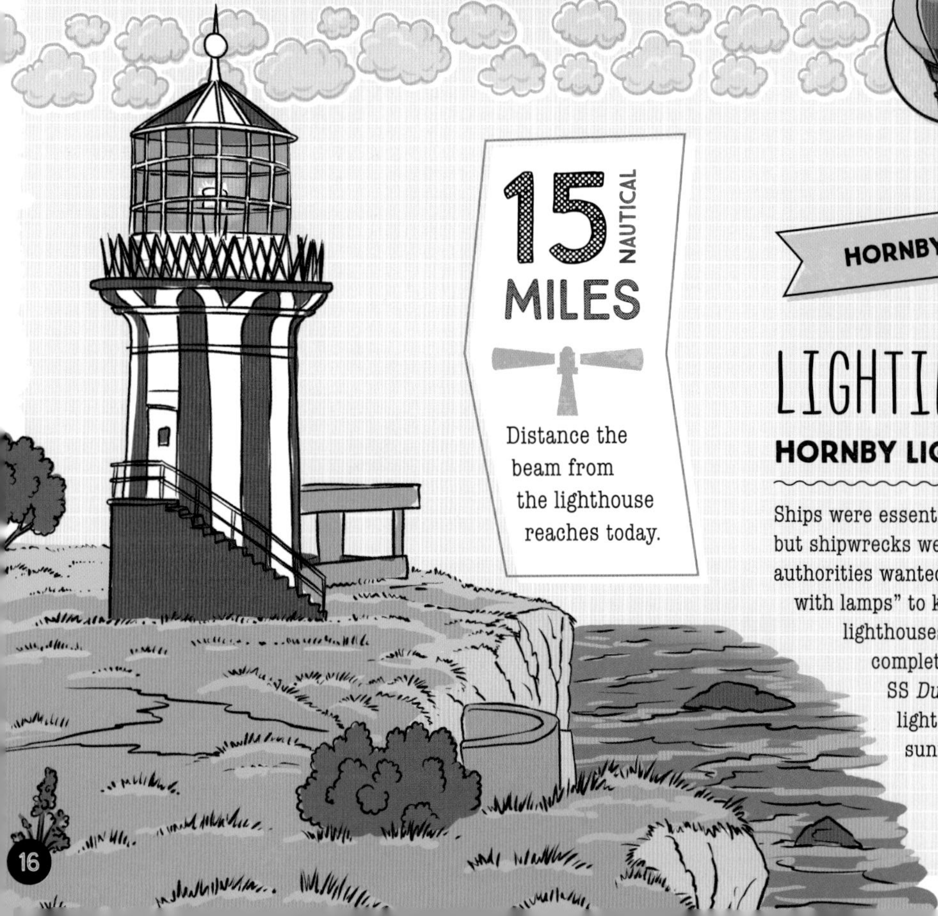

15 NAUTICAL MILES

Distance the beam from the lighthouse reaches today.

HORNBY LIGHTHOUSE

LIGHTING THE WAY

HORNBY LIGHTHOUSE

Ships were essential to Australian trade in the 19th century, but shipwrecks were on the increase. Worried New South Wales authorities wanted to light the coastal skyline "like a street with lamps" to keep ships safe. Between 1858 and 1903, 13 lighthouses were built. Hornby was one of the first, completed in 1858 as a direct result of the wreck of the SS *Dunbar* the year before (see page 13). Today, the light is automated, but it's a great place to see the sunrise and maybe spot a whale or two.

3.3 FT.
(1 M)
Average width of a
flying fox's wings.

SYDNEY SEAP...
WWW.SEAPLANES.COM.AU

VH-AAM

FLYING PICNIC

ROSE BAY

Sydney's first international airport was at Rose Bay. It was a "water airport" for planes that could land on water or on the ground. In 1938, Empire Flying Boats traveled between Sydney and England. It was a ten-day luxury trip, landing nine times for passengers to sleep and 20 times to refuel the plane. The views of the harbor were especially splendid from this plane, because it rarely rose above 5,000 ft. (1.5 km). Smaller seaplanes fly here today, and some trips even pack a picnic, but they won't fly much further than Barrenjoey Lighthouse.

VAMPIRE-WATCH

WOLLI CREEK VALLEY

They're sometimes called vampires or winged devils, but flying fox is this animal's real name, and it isn't going to bite. In fact, these creatures aren't even foxes, they're big bats. During the daytime, they hang upside down together in colonies, but just after sunset, they fly out to search for food – in their thousands! It's quite a sight.

**AU$322
(US$240)**
Cost of a one-way ticket – about as much as most people earned in a year!

15
Number of passengers on board.

160 MPH
(258 KM/H)
The speed of travel.

40 DAYS
How long the same trip took by ship.

WOLLI CREEK VALLEY

ROSE BAY

MAKING A SPLASH

With temperatures in the city soaring above 82°F (28°C) in January, and dropping no lower than 45°F (7°C) in July, some hardy Sydneysiders take to the water all year round. There are plenty of pools to choose from, not to mention the beaches...

CLEAN AND GREEN

PRINCE ALFRED PARK POOL

This pool was looking quite shabby when the architects were called in. Given strict instructions not to lose too much of the surrounding park, they designed an invisible poolside building, which is cleverly disguised as a lawn! Stylish yellow umbrellas keep the bathers in the shade, and heated water makes this the perfect place for local folks to enjoy a year-round dip.

START

PRINCE ALFRED PARK POOL

COOLING OFF

SYDNEY OLYMPIC PARK AQUATIC CENTRE

Swimming, diving, water polo, and synchronized swimming competitions took place here during the 2000 Olympics (see pages 74–75). Since then, the water park has welcomed the public to enjoy the four pools, along with a giant waterslide, rapid river ride, spa, sauna, and steam rooms.

SYDNEY OLYMPIC PARK AQUATIC CENTRE

MORE THAN 35,000 PLANTS GROW ON PRINCE ALFRED PARK POOL'S GREEN ROOFTOP, MAKING IT THE BIGGEST OF ITS KIND IN THE CITY.

WATER UNDER THE BRIDGE

NORTH SYDNEY OLYMPIC POOL

Swimming the backstroke in this pool, as trains rattle overhead, is an amazing way to see the Sydney Harbour Bridge next door. Opened in 1936, the pool's clean water earned it the nickname the "Wonder Pool." Swimming and diving events for the 1938 Empire Games took place here. An impressive 86 world records have been broken in these waters.

NORTH SYDNEY OLYMPIC POOL

MACCALLUM POOL

A SECRET SWIM

MACCALLUM POOL

A short ferry trip across the harbor leads those in the know to this hidden seawater pool. It started life as a rock pool, hollowed out by Fred Lane, Oz's first Olympic swimming champ. Fred won gold in the 200 m freestyle at the Paris 1900 Olympics, setting a world record that held for 68 years! He retired in 1902, aged just 22.

HOW IT ALL BEGAN...

FRESHWATER BEACH

Freshie, as it's known to the locals, gets its name from the freshwater creek that flows down onto the beach below. People flocked here to swim in the 1900s. In 1915, crowds gathered for a visit from the Hawaiian surf-swimming champion Duke Kahanamoku. The Duke arrived carrying a specially designed surfboard; minds were blown as the spectators watched him ride the waves, and an Australian craze was born.

THIRTY THOUSAND NSW KIDS AGED 5–13 ARE ENCOURAGED TO BECOME "NIPPERS" AND LEARN SURF SAFETY. THE EMPHASIS IS ON FUN, BUT THE MESSAGE IS SERIOUS: ONCE THEY'RE TRAINED, THESE KIDS CAN SAVE LIVES.

FRESHWATER BEACH

SURF'S UP

MANLY BEACH

Swimming in the daytime was forbidden on Manly until 1903, but attitudes change fast, and by 1909, the Manly Life Saving Club claims their beach had the first Aussie surfer. Early boards were very long and incredibly heavy; it wasn't until the 1950s that lightweight balsa-wood boards arrived. The first-ever World Surfing Championships happened here in 1964, and Manly still hosts the Australian Open of Surfing at the end of February each year.

MANLY BEACH

FROM SEA TO SCREEN

BONDI PAVILION

Even the most ardent surfers can't stay in the water all the time, but they might take a break to watch movies about it. Sydney's first Surf Film Festival took place in 2015 and included stunning documentaries such as *The Cradle of Storms*, about the journey three surfers took to Alaska to ride some previously untamed ice-cold waves. Brrr!

ART GALLERY NSW

ART OF THE BEACH

ART GALLERY NSW

In Sydney, you don't have to go to the beach to appreciate it. Works about beach life are often on display in the Art Gallery of New South Wales, including some by Max Dupain, one of Australia's best-loved photographers. Max's most famous photograph, *Sunbaker*, was taken in 1937 and became one of Australia's most famous images. In 2016, a collection of Max's prints sold at auction for a record-breaking AU$1 million (US$750,000), with *Sunbaker* (right) selling for AU$85,000 (US$63,000).

"Reckon I'll be rich one day!"

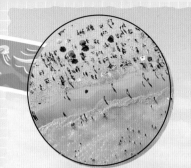

FUN ON BONDI BEACH

SOUNDS OF THE SURF

"Bondi" is an Aboriginal word to describe the noise waves make when they crash over rocks. The huge waves here are still legendary today. In fact, this is Australia's most famous beach — it even features in its own TV series, *Bondi Rescue*.

BONDI BEACH

SKATE ON THE BEACH

It's not just surfers who head to Bondi, though. There are sections of the beach for families and swimmers, too. You can even skate here in July, when the biggest seaside ice skating rink in the southern hemisphere touches down for two weeks.

DANGEROUS CURRENT

LOOK OUT, LOOK OUT!

More menacing than sharks is the vicious Bondi riptide that can sweep swimmers up to 1,312 ft. (400 m) out to sea faster than an Olympic champion. Locals know how to spot the powerful current, and warning signs alert visitors to the danger.

Lifeguards say if you're carried off by a riptide:

- **Keep calm.**
- **Float to save energy or swim gently, parallel to the beach, towards white water.**
- **Don't fight against the current.**
- **Raise an arm to get attention.**

SEASIDE RIDE

In 2016, camels visited the beach to offer rides. Although an unusual sight on Bondi, camels came to Australia in the 1800s. They were used to carry heavy loads in the outback, but set free when vehicles took over. Oz now has up to 750,000 wild camels — more than anywhere else in the world!

SURFING SANTA

In December 2015, a Guinness World Record was broken for the largest-ever surfing lesson when 320 surfers hit Bondi Beach — every one of them dressed in a Santa suit!

ICEBERG SWIMMERS

BONDI'S OUTDOOR BEACH POOL IS NICKNAMED "ICEBERGS" AFTER THE CLUB THAT'S BASED THERE. MEMBERS RACE HERE ON SUNDAYS ALL YEAR ROUND, WHATEVER THE WEATHER — NO WET SUITS ALLOWED — AND FROM MAY TO SEPTEMBER, IT CAN GET PRETTY CHILLY! PLUS, THE POOL'S RIGHT NEXT TO THE SEA, SO WAVES REGULARLY CRASH OVER ITS SIDES.

search: BONDI BEACH POOL

📍 JUNIOR CLUB

Bondi Icecubes is the largest junior winter swimming club in Australia. On wintry Sunday mornings, spurred on by the thought of a free sausage sandwich, young "Icecubes" race the 164 ft. (50 m) length of the Icebergs outdoor pool.

CITY SPOOKS

Sydney has its fair share of dark tales, urban myths, and shadowy stories. See how many of the ghoulish yarns you believe on this trail...

START

WAKEHURST PARKWAY

GHOUL POWER

MANLY QUARANTINE STATION

Over 500 people died of terrible diseases when the Quarantine Station was open. Today, it's one of Oz's most haunted sites. If you're feeling brave enough, you can join an after-dark ghost tour. Take care in the dining area, though. It's said to be haunted by two little girls; one is helpful, the other is not. More than one visitor has felt the unhelpful ghost pulling them towards the floor, trying to grab their neck – eek!

MANLY QUARANTINE STATION

WHO'S IN THE BACK?

WAKEHURST PARKWAY

Police warn drivers to avoid this road after dark. It's said that around midnight, "Kelly" can suddenly appear in the back seat of a car. If the driver doesn't tell her to go away, this little girl may make them veer right off the road! With no streetlights and dense forest on either side, this stretch of Wakehurst Parkway is pitch black so there are loads of accidents here. But is that due to the dark... or something more sinister?

THE ROCKS' ARGYLE CUT GANG OFTEN HIT THEIR VICTIMS ON THE HEAD WITH A SOCK FULL OF WET SAND! IF THE COPS CAME CHASING, THEY'D HIDE THE EVIDENCE BY EMPTYING THE SOCK AND SLIPPING IT ON THEIR FOOT.

In 2014, bottles and glasses began falling to the floor of the Carlisle Castle Hotel when no one was around to drop them. This was a ghost with specific tastes – it preferred wine, and only the more expensive bottles!

ROUGH TIMES

CADMAN'S COTTAGE

The Rocks is the oldest part of Sydney, and the first European settlement in the whole of Australia. Its first residents were convicts and, in the 19th century, gangs of youths roamed the filthy streets. Muggings were common. There were murders, too, and even an outbreak of bubonic plague! So there are spooks aplenty here, from the body found in a suitcase on the steps of Cadman's Cottage to the mysterious faces that appear in some windows of old buildings late at night.

TINKLING KEYS

THE HERO OF WATERLOO

This old pub was built in 1843 and comes complete with a secret tunnel for rum smuggling. In 1849, the landlord murdered his wife in the pub by pushing her down the stairs. Now, chairs change position overnight, and sometimes a mysterious tinkling music comes from the piano, even if its lid was left firmly shut.

HERO OF WATERLOO

THE HERO OF WATERLOO

RATTLING CHAINS

SYDNEY HARBOUR BRIDGE

Perhaps a ghostly rattling sound reported on Australia's most famous bridge is actually the eerie clanging of phantom steel cables, like those used during its construction. Records show that 16 workers died while building the bridge, but according to legend, three more were not accounted for. Because these workers were not registered, their deaths were never acknowledged, and their bodies were never found.

SYDNEY HARBOUR BRIDGE

KINSELAS

DANCING WITH DEATH

KINSELAS

From its warm, friendly atmosphere, customers would never guess that this food, drink, and dance venue was once a funeral parlor for nearly 50 years! Charles Kinsela was a thoroughly modern undertaker (the first in Sydney to introduce funerals with motorized transportation), who had this building lavishly redesigned in 1930s Art Deco style, to suit new trends in funerals.

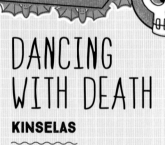

UP TO 1,900 funerals at Kinselas each year in the 1930s.

COFFIN CARRIAGE

MORTUARY STATION

When cemeteries in the center of Sydney started to fill up, officials decided to send the dead to a leafier resting place, with fountains, flower beds, and neat pathways. So Mortuary Station opened in 1869, and mourners from the city paid a shilling each way for tickets to see their loved ones off at the new cemetery. Coffins traveled free in a specially built wagon, but of course they only went one way.

DO-GOODING GHOST

CAMPERDOWN CEMETERY

A memorial at this cemetery commemorates Mrs. Bathsheba Ghost (yes, really – a ghost called Ghost!), who was transported to Sydney from London to serve a sentence of 14 years. She was freed after just six years, became a nurse at the Sydney Infirmary and Dispensary, and quickly rose through the ranks to become matron in charge. She died at her place of work and some say she still leaves her Camperdown grave to tend to the sick.

CAMPERDOWN CEMETERY

15,000 BODIES

buried in Camperdown Cemetery from 1849 to 1868. Half of those were placed in unmarked graves.

12 BODIES

buried each day during one vicious 19th-century measles epidemic.

THE CITY'S SETTLERS

Sydney's population has its origins in many parts of the world, and these immigrants have plenty of fascinating and varied stories to tell.

HARD LIFE

HYDE PARK BARRACKS

HYDE PARK BARRACKS

In the 18th century, prisons were expensive and difficult places to manage, and the death penalty couldn't deal with every crime. If a convict was fit to work, they could actually be useful. That's why British courts started sending their criminals off to build new colonies. At first, offenders were shipped off to work in America, but in 1783, America won its independence from Britain, and the convicts had to go somewhere else.

A LUKEWARM WELCOME

Once the convicts arrived in Sydney, they were marched to the barracks and given work. Men with useful skills could stay put, while others had to labor in quarries and on construction sites. Women often worked as housemaids. The barracks weren't a prison, but those who stayed suffered harsh rules, strict timetables, and no privacy.

THE BARRACKS, BUILT FOR 600 CONVI OFTEN HOUSED 1,400

HARD LUCK!

Famous barracks resident James Hardy Vaux was sent to Australia for seven years for pickpocketing, swindling, and gambling. He served his sentence and returned home, where he robbed a shop. He was then shipped to Sydney for life! Vaux got off early for good behavior and traveled home but was arrested for carrying fake banknotes. Back in Australia, he wrote a book on convict slang.

NOT PRISON BUT...

- A bell rang to wake residents in time to start work at sunrise.

- They worked until sunset, only breaking for lunch if it was really hot.

- The bell also rang at mealtime, inspection time, and bedtime.

- Everyone washed their clothes on Saturdays. Those with a dirty shirt at Sunday's inspection were fined.

- Beds were rough linen hammocks hung in large, shared dormitories.

A STROKE OF THE CAT

CONVICTS WHO BEHAVED THEMSELVES AND WORKED HARD COULD EARN THEIR FREEDOM AND EVEN PASSAGE HOME. FOR THOSE WHO DIDN'T BEHAVE, THERE WERE SOME NASTY PUNISHMENTS: SWEARING, LAZINESS, DRUNKENNESS, LATENESS, AND PETTY THIEVING COULD EARN THEM A LASHING WITH THE CAT-O'-NINE-TAILS (A WHIP WITH NINE LENGTHS OF KNOTTED ROPE).

NO ESCAPE?

COCKATOO ISLAND

Only the worst offenders were sent here – and the ones who couldn't behave themselves at the barracks. From 1839 to 1869, this island was used as a prison. The task of the first inmates? To construct their own prison building. They went on to carve out a dry dock for shipbuilding and underground grain stores – all without the help of machinery. Life was tough, and escape was impossible – almost...

IN 1864, FRED WARD AND FRED BRITTEN ESCAPED FROM THE ISLAND BY SWIMMING TO THE MAINLAND. WARD BECAME A NOTORIOUS OUTLAW, WHO WENT BY THE NAME OF CAPTAIN THUNDERBOLT, UNTIL HE WAS SHOT AND KILLED BY AN OFF-DUTY POLICEMAN IN 1870.

"I want to go home!"

COCKATOO ISLAND

ST. JAMES' CHURCH

BUILDING A CAREER

ST. JAMES' CHURCH

Escaping a death sentence for forgery, Francis Greenway was transported in 1813 to serve a 14-year sentence. He quite probably thought his life was over anyway, but when the Governor of New South Wales (NSW) discovered he was an architect, Francis was allowed to start work right away. He designed houses, lighthouses, monuments, forts, and churches (such as this one), many of which are still standing today.

45,000
GALLONS OF RUM
How much the hospital cost.

200
The number of hospital beds provided.

A RUM DEAL

SYDNEY MINT

Once known as the Rum Hospital, this building treated sick convicts between 1816 and 1848 before becoming the Sydney Mint. The governor of NSW had no money at the time, so he'd paid for the building with rum! Back then, it had a more sinister nickname, too — the Sydney Slaughterhouse. Brutal treatments, such as blood-letting, and the toxic medicines prescribed here were often deadly!

SYDNEY MINT

A SINISTER SWING

FORT DENISON

Some still call this island fort by its 18th-century nickname of "Pinchgut." Before the fort was built, it was just a rocky island prison reserved for hardened criminals who might be kept in chains on a diet of bread and water. Prisoner Francis Morgan was hanged here for murder in 1796, and his body was left swinging in the breeze for four years as a warning!

Try talking like a convict:
- Galloot/Swoddy – Soldier
- Horney – Constable
- Knuckler – Pickpocket
- Scamp – Highway robber

31

POM — AUSSIE NICKNAME FOR AN ENGLISH PERSON. POSSIBLY BECAUSE ENGLISH SKIN TURNS RED, LIKE A POMEGRANATE, IN THE SUN!

1 MILLION+
Ten Pound Poms stayed in Oz.

250,000
of them returned to Britain.

ABOUT **125,000**
of those went back again to Oz!

A HARSH VOYAGE

SYDNEY JEWISH MUSEUM

This museum tells stories from Jewish Holocaust survivors who settled in Sydney after World War II. But, during the war, Jews came here for a different reason. In 1940, Britain began treating Germans, Italians, and Austrians as "enemy aliens." Over 2,500 were crammed as prisoners onto a ship bound for Australia. Most were not Nazis — two-thirds were Jewish refugees escaping the brutal regime! On arrival in Sydney, around 2,000 men were moved to prison camps. The British eventually apologized, but about 900 "prisoners" ended up settling in Oz.

BOOMERANG POMS

OVERSEAS PASSENGER TERMINAL

After World War II, Australia desperately needed workers. A special deal was struck so that British citizens could come and live here for £10 (US$13), but they had to stay for two years, or pay back the fare in full. Thousands boarded British emigration ships and arrived at Sydney's Overseas Passenger Terminal. Some made the most of the opportunity; others sat tight for two years, then headed home. But the "Boomerang Poms" got home, realized they preferred Oz, and came back again!

16 Jews arrived with the first 1,500 convicts.

27,000 Jewish Holocaust survivors immigrated to Australia after World War II.

OVERSEAS PASSENGER TERMINAL

CABRAMATTA

EXCELLENT TASTE

CABRAMATTA

In 1978, Vietnamese refugees started arriving in Sydney to escape Vietnam's communist regime. By 2006, the city had 72,615 Vietnamese speakers. Many started their Australian life in the Cabramatta Migrant Hostel. When they moved from here, they often settled nearby. Vietnamese shops and restaurants soon opened up, and today this area is a foodie's paradise. How about trying vegetable fries with sugar syrup, mung-bean donuts, or a jackfruit-and-lychee shake?

> VIETNAMESE IS SYDNEY'S FIFTH LANGUAGE — NEARLY 2 PERCENT OF THE POPULATION IS FROM VIETNAM.

ITALY IN OZ

NORTON STREET

Locals know this area as Little Italy, and for the last 30 years, an Italian festival has happened here each year. With 125,000 visitors, it's now the largest community street festival in Australia. Attractions include Italian cars, scooters, fashion, and food. Italians have been coming to Oz since the 1820s, searching for a better life, but bringing their best traditions with them.

NORTON STREET

THE NAME GAME

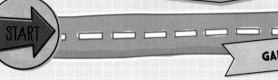

Sydney's place names tell us a lot about its history. The city itself is named after the English politician who first sent convicts to Botany Bay, even though he wasn't actually called Sydney. He was born Thomas Townshend, but was made "Baron Sydney" by the British king in 1783. British settlers gave many Australian places names from home, so Sydney has a "Liverpool," a "Kings Cross," and a "Hyde Park."

START

GARDEN ISLAND

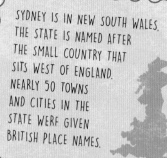

SYDNEY IS IN NEW SOUTH WALES. THE STATE IS NAMED AFTER THE SMALL COUNTRY THAT SITS WEST OF ENGLAND. NEARLY 50 TOWNS AND CITIES IN THE STATE WERE GIVEN BRITISH PLACE NAMES.

NOT-SO-GORGEOUS GARDEN

GARDEN ISLAND

Despite its name, Garden Island isn't a garden or an island, but once upon a time it was both. After the First Fleet landed, it was quickly planted to grow food for sailors on HMS *Sirius*, one of the fleet's ships. During World War II, land was reclaimed to join the island to the mainland. Today, it's an Australian naval base.

THE ISLAND LAYS CLAIM TO AUSTRALIA'S EARLIEST EXAMPLE OF A SETTLER'S GRAFFITI. THE RATHER UNIMAGINATIVE "FM 1788" WAS ETCHED INTO THE ROCK BY FREDERICK MEREDITH, A STEWARD ABOARD HMS *SIRIUS*.

FM 1788

STINK OR SWIM?

COOGEE BEACH

Tourists might not be so keen to visit this beautiful, surf-friendly, sandy beach and plunge into its glistening waters if they knew what the word "coogee" really meant. Local Aboriginal people called the beach "koojah," which translates as "smelly place," or "koo-chai," which very precisely identifies the smell as "stinking seaweed."

COOGEE BEACH

GUESS THE MEANING

WOOLLOOMOOLOO FINGER WHARF

Traditionally, Woolloomooloo was one of the poorer areas of Sydney, but this 1,312 ft. (400 m) long wharf has been redeveloped as apartments for the rich and famous. The shape of the wharf gives the "finger" part of the name, but nobody agrees on the Aboriginal origins of "Woolloomooloo." Different translations say it means: "place of plenty," "field of blood," or "young black kangaroo."

AU$30 MILLION
(US$22 MILLION)

Estimated value of actor Russell Crowe's luxury Finger Wharf apartment in 2016.

WOOLLOOMOOLOO FINGER WHARF

WEDDING CAKE ISLAND

A ROCKY PROPOSAL

WEDDING CAKE ISLAND

When waves crash onto this rocky island, it looks like the icing on a wedding cake. It's the perfect place to propose. Things didn't go to plan, though, for Sydneyside couple Hilton and Talia. Hilton's boat ran out of fuel on the way to the island, and he fell into the water on the way back. Lifeguards had to rescue him twice! But he did manage to pop the question, and luckily, Talia said, "Yes."

AU$6 BILLION
(US$4.5 BILLION)
Cost of redeveloping Barangaroo.

75,000
shrubs and trees are being planted in the Barangaroo Reserve.

LEGENDARY LADY

BARANGAROO

This area is Sydney's newest suburb and even has its own wildlife reserve, though the whole project won't be finished until 2024. For years the site was used for shipping and didn't look too pretty, but long before that it was owned by the Cammeraygal people, who fished and hunted here for over 6,000 years. Barangaroo was a highly respected fisherwoman who wouldn't take any nonsense from the interfering Europeans.

BARANGAROO

BLUES POINT

TOP HAT AND TALES

BLUES POINT

Billy Blue was well known for his tatty top hat and witty banter. He probably came from Jamaica, but was transported from London for stealing sugar. Billy served his time and progressed from oyster-seller to harbor watchman and owning his own land and a fleet of ferries. He was accused of smuggling and even manslaughter, but he hung onto his land and it's still called Blues Point today.

ABORIGINAL SYDNEYSIDERS HAD A NAME FOR THE TIP OF THIS PENINSULA LONG BEFORE BILLY BLUE CAME ALONG. THEY STILL CALL IT WARUNGAREEYUH TO THIS DAY. THE VIEWS FROM BLUES POINT ARE SOME OF THE BEST IN THE WHOLE OF THE CITY.

NAMED AND CLAIMED
MANLY

When Arthur Phillip, the first governor of Sydney, explored Port Jackson, he was particularly impressed by the "confidence and manly behavior" of a group of Aboriginal people in the north of the bay. The men were going about their business – as they had done for thousands of years. Phillip had no claim over the area, but he named it Manly Cove anyway, and it wasn't long before a plan was drawn up to build a township there.

MANLY

A BIT HAZY
BLUE MOUNTAINS

The Blue Mountains are so called because, well, they look blue – or, at least, they give off a blue haze. The haze is caused by fine droplets of oil from the huge eucalyptus trees, which are densely packed on the mountainsides. See page 48 for more info.

THE WOLLEMI PINE TREES DISCOVERED IN THE MOUNTAINS IN 1994 GROW UP TO 131 FT. (40 M) HIGH. BEFORE THEIR DISCOVERY, SCIENTISTS ONLY KNEW THE TREES FROM FOSSILIZED SAMPLES THAT WERE 60 MILLION YEARS OLD!

BLUE MOUNTAINS

SYDNEY SHAPES

With Sydney Harbour Bridge and the Opera House, the city's skyline is easy to recognize, but there are plenty more shapes that aren't so well known.

START

CLOUD ARCH
GEORGE STREET

Japanese artist Junya Ishigami plans to build a 164 ft. (50 m) high steel sculpture in the heart of the city. He says it's all about cloud technology and connections, but just like a cloud in the sky, the shape of *Cloud Arch* will change depending on where people view it from. Fans call it an elegant gateway; critics say it looks like dental floss or a rubber band.

GEORGE STREET

ART GALLERY OF NEW SOUTH WALES

ALMOST ONCE
ART GALLERY OF NEW SOUTH WALES

Brett Whiteley was one of Oz's best-known artists. He gave this 26 ft. (8 m) high sculpture called *Almost Once* to the gallery in 1991. Ever since, passers-by have tried to figure out what the burnt match next to the unused match means. The local cockatoos don't care – they use the burnt match to sharpen their beaks on!

search: PYRAMID TOWER

PYRAMID TOWER

This 62 ft. (19 m) tall sculpture is a tower of shiny pyramid shapes plonked on top of one another. Pyramid Tower is designed to blend in with surrounding skyscrapers, but some Sydneysiders aren't impressed; they call it the "Shish Kebab"!

ROUND AND ROUND

O BAR AND DINING

On the 47th floor of Australia Square is a rather swanky restaurant. The *O* in the name is a clue to its shape as, yes, this restaurant is completely round. There are great views of the city below, and customers don't need to cross the room to catch the view on the other side, because the whole restaurant revolves!

Australia Square

PUDDING BOWL

BLUE MOUNTAINS

English writer Philip Pullman calls *The Magic Pudding* "the funniest children's book ever written." It's all about a walking, talking, edible pudding, called Albert. The author and illustrator Norman Lindsay lived in the Blue Mountains. He wrote *The Magic Pudding* to prove to a friend that children liked reading books about food and fighting better than ones about fairies. It is even divided into slices instead of chapters! The book was first published in 1918, and it's still in print today.

BLUE MOUNTAINS

A LOT OF BOTTLE

ROYAL BOTANIC GARDEN

This strange-looking tree is known as a bottle tree because of its peculiarly bulbous bottle shape. The tree grows straight when it's young, but between the ages of five and eight years, it starts to look like it's putting on weight. In fact, the tree's storing water in case of a drought — so it's a bottle in more ways than one! One very elderly bottle tree in the Botanic Garden has been growing here since 1846!

65 FT. (20 M)
Height of the tallest bottle trees.
The hotter the climate,
the taller they grow.

THERE'S ALSO A BOTTLE-BRUSH TREE WITH BRIGHTLY COLORED FLOWERS SHAPED LIKE, YOU GUESSED IT, A BOTTLE BRUSH.

ROYAL BOTANIC GARDEN

IAN THORPE AQUATIC CENTRE

MAKING WAVES

IAN THORPE AQUATIC CENTRE

This spectacular swimming pool has won awards for its architecture, with its curved roof designed in the shape of a wave on the ocean. Inside and out it looks amazing, but the staff in the building isn't all that keen on it. They say the curve means there's only half the pool space there should be, the gym is too small, and chemicals in the water are causing the walls to corrode!

AU$40 MILLION
(US$30 MILLION)
How much the Ian Thorpe Aquatic
Centre cost to build in 2007.

FIRE AND WATER

SYDNEY OLYMPIC PARK

Kids love to play in this water feature that's shaped like a UFO on stilts, but back in 2000 it had a really important role to play in the Olympic Games. This was the cauldron lit by Cathy Freeman (see page 75) at the start of the games. The flame rose up above her head and traveled to the top of the stadium, where it burned for the rest of the games.

SYDNEY OLYMPIC PARK

UNIVERSITY OF TECHNOLOGY AND SCIENCE

PAPER BAG BUILDING

UNIVERSITY OF TECHNOLOGY AND SCIENCE

Architect Frank Gehry took his design ideas for this business school building from a tree house. It's built from specially made bricks, all laid by hand, and colored to match Sydney's older buildings. Inside, classrooms are oval, and lecture halls are curved. When someone joked that the building looked like a squashed brown paper bag, Oz's governor general said it's "the most beautiful squashed brown paper bag I've ever seen."

320,000
BRICKS AND GLASS PANELS

AU$180 MILLION (US$133 MILLION)
Cost of building the paper-bag-shaped university.

MUSICAL SAILS

SYDNEY OPERA HOUSE

The Sydney Opera House is probably this city's most famous shape. Today, it's hard to imagine the harbor without it, but back in the 1960s, many people thought it might never be finished.

8.2 MILLION VISITORS EACH YEAR

2,000 PERFORMANCES ARE HOSTED EVERY YEAR

LISTEN WHILE YOU WORK

The first-ever performance at the Opera House happened before it even opened. Famous African American singer, actor, and megastar Paul Robeson gave a free performance to more than 250 workers who watched from the scaffolding on the construction site.

SYDNEY OPERA HOUSE

STIFF COMPETITION

In 1956, Sydney's government held a competition to design an opera house, and 220 entries flooded in! At first, Danishman Jørn Utzon's design was rejected, but a new judge declared it a masterpiece. Jørn hadn't been to Sydney, but he knew about boats and the sea. He wanted the building to blend in with its harbor setting — so he designed the roof to look like yacht sails.

SOMETHING TO SING ABOUT

The story of the building of Sydney Opera House is so fascinating that, in 1995, an opera was written about it! In 2016, *The Eighth Wonder* was performed outside the Opera House, with giant screens and moving scenery helping to tell the story. The performers sang live, while music was piped to 3,500 spectators through special headphones that cut out background noise.

HUT TO HOUSE

THE OPERA HOUSE SITS ON BENNELONG POINT, WHERE WOOLLARAWARRE BENNELONG'S SMALL HUT ONCE STOOD. BENNELONG WAS AN ABORIGINAL MAN, WHO WAS CAPTURED, LEARNED ENGLISH, AND TRAVELED TO ENGLAND TO MEET KING GEORGE III.

WRENCH IN THE WORKS

In 1965, the shell roof was nearly complete, but costs had grown. A new government took office and refused to pay up. Jørn was forced to resign, but new architects were employed to finish the building. Their redesigns were much more costly, yet one singer claimed the opera stage was the size of a handkerchief!

WHEN THE OPERA HOUSE TURNED 40, IN 2013, IT HAD A MONTH-LONG PARTY OF EVENTS AND A GIANT BIRTHDAY CUPCAKE. AS PART OF THE CELEBRATIONS, 6,000 REGULAR-SIZED CAKES WERE GIVEN AWAY.

6 PERFORMANCE VENUES INSIDE!

search: OPERA HOUSE

IT TOOK:

📍 **16 YEARS** to build. Work started in 1957 and was completed in 1973.

📍 **4 YEARS** to figure out how to build the roof shells.

📍 **3 YEARS** to weave two of the inside curtains.

📍 **1 YEAR** to develop the tiles that cover the shells — over 1 million were made.

GO OUTDOORS

When the sun shines 340 days of the year, it's good to explore the great outdoors, and in Sydney there are plenty of things to keep you entertained all day long.

OODLES OF NIGHTTIME NOODLES

HYDE PARK

For 18 nights in October, the Night Noodle Market is in business, and this park turns into an open-air restaurant. Beneath its twinkling lights, and amid sensational smells, some of Sydney's best eating establishments show off their tastiest Asian dishes, with cooking demos, live DJs, musicians, and even ping-pong on the side. Mmm...

DANCING IN THE PARK

ROYAL BOTANIC GARDEN

The plants in this park come from all corners of the world, and there are nearly 4,000 trees in the gardens and surrounding area, many of them fig trees. This Moreton Bay fig tree is one of the oldest and widest of all the fig trees. It's nicknamed the "Children's Fig" because children used to love clambering on it. Sadly, it's now fenced off for protection, but little ones can get up and dance on Tuesdays and Fridays at the Botanic Beats disco.

OVER
3.5 MILLION
people visit the Botanic Garden each year.

START

HYDE PARK

ROYAL BOTANIC GARDEN

MOVIE MAGIC

ST. GEORGE OPEN AIR CINEMA

It might be difficult to peel your eyes away
from the backdrop when watching a movie here.
St. George doesn't call itself "the most beautiful
cinema in the world" for nothing. Its 2,000 seats
face the Sydney skyline, with the Opera House and
Harbour Bridge straight ahead. As the sky grows dark,
the three-story-high screen rises! With 32 speakers,
the audience is wrapped up in the show and the warmth
of the summer evening skies.

IF IT RAINS DURING A
SHOW, EVERYONE GETS
A FREE PLASTIC PONCHO.

CHRISTMAS
ON THE BEACH

SHELLY BEACH

Christmas comes at the beginning of the Australian
school summer vacation, so loads of people head for
the beach. Family-friendly Shelly Beach has BBQs you
can borrow, though you'll probably roast prawns, not
chestnuts (traditional Christmas lunch these days
is cold turkey and salad). Most people are dressed
for a dip or snorkel in the sea, but they might add
a Santa hat and beard. In Oz, even Santa wears
shorts, and his sleigh might be pulled by kangaroos.

40,000 PEOPLE ARE LIKELY TO HEAD
TO BONDI BEACH ON CHRISTMAS DAY.
THERE'LL BE A CHRISTMAS TREE
ON THE BEACH AND PLENTY OF
SNOWMEN — MADE OUT OF SAND!

SHELLY BEACH

45

SHHH, IT'S A SECRET

FOUNDATION PARK, THE ROCKS

This park's not signposted, and you get there via a maze of narrow streets, then through an anonymous doorway. On the other side of the door lie the remains of eight townhouses that date back to the 1870s. The houses were knocked down in 1938, but the roofless foundation walls are still standing. The old-fashioned furniture models show how cramped the rooms were in this poor, rough area. It's an eerie open-air museum.

IN THE 1970S, THERE WERE PLANS TO FLATTEN THE OLD HOUSES AND REPLACE THEM WITH OFFICE BUILDINGS. LUCKILY, LOCALS CAMPAIGNED TO SAVE THEM, AS THE ROCKS IS NOW ONE OF SYDNEY'S MOST POPULAR TOURIST ATTRACTIONS.

10 SQ. FT.

The size of the rooms in the old, ruined houses.

FOUNDATION PARK

RUSHCUTTERS BAY PARK

KEEP ON RUNNING

RUSHCUTTERS BAY PARK

Instead of running on a treadmill and staring at a wall, Sydneysiders have a great choice of outdoor gyms. This one has the best view: straight across the harbor with a selection of beautiful boats to gaze at.

RUSHCUTTERS BAY PARK STANDS ON RECLAIMED LAND WHERE WETLAND REEDS WERE ONCE ABUNDANT. EARLY SETTLERS USED THESE REEDS, OR RUSHES, TO THATCH THE ROOFS OF THEIR HOUSES, AND THE "RUSH CUTTERS" WHO COLLECTED THEM GAVE THEIR NAME TO THE AREA.

BAREFOOT IN THE PARK
CLOVELLY BOWLING CLUB

Traditionally, lawn bowling was seen as an old people's game, with its stiff white uniforms and strict rules. That is until someone had the bright idea of jazzing up the sport a bit to appeal to a younger crowd. Barefoot Bowls is a more relaxed game that's all about having fun. Players wear what they like, though a sun hat is recommended, and they're welcome to take off their shoes. What better excuse for a BBQ, too?

180 birdcages are suspended above the street.

THE GAME IS PLAYED WITH TWO TEAMS, TWO SETS OF COLORED BALLS, AND A SMALLER "JACK," WHICH IS PLACED ON THE LAWN. TEAMS TAKE TURNS TO ROLL THEIR BALLS. THE ONE THAT GETS ITS BALLS CLOSEST TO THE JACK WINS POINTS.

CLOVELLY BOWLING CLUB

OUTDOOR TWEETING
ANGEL PLACE

When visitors turn down this alleyway, they'll notice the sound first. Invisible birds twitter here all day long, their song changing according to the time of day. Empty cages dangle above pedestrians' heads, and the names of bird species that once lived here are etched in the stone under their feet. It's a work of art, installed in 2009, and the tweets are recordings. The piece was supposed to be temporary, but Sydneysiders loved it so much they asked for it to stay.

BIG BLUE WONDER

THE BLUE MOUNTAINS

It's a short 31-mile (50-km) journey inland from Sydney to the Blue Mountains. The scenery here is fabulous, with rocky outcrops, stunning views, spectacular waterfalls, rolling rivers, deep caves, and far-reaching forests. The area is so special, it's now protected as a UNESCO World Heritage site.

BLACK CAT MYSTERY

Australia doesn't have its own big cat, but many locals here say there's a family of pumas living deep in the forest. Others disagree – how would the animals have got there? Well, there are many theories:

➡ They came to guard the gold mines of the 1850s.
➡ They were the exotic pets of American WWII servicemen.
➡ They're descendants of a meat-eating lion with a pouch that lived here 1.6 million years ago – and died out 40,000 years ago.

UNDERGROUND STARS

A dark, damp, abandoned railway tunnel hidden beneath 590 ft. (180 m) of rock is the perfect place to spot glowworms. A curve in the railway line means part of this tunnel is especially dark. Visitors need to be super-quiet, turn off their flashlights, and stand very still to see the walls light up like stars in the sky.

THE BLUE MOUNTAINS

THE THREE SISTERS

This stunning rock formation gets its name from an Aboriginal legend: three sisters from one tribe fell in love with three brothers from another. When their marriages were forbidden, the couples tried to run away and a battle broke out. A witch doctor protected the sisters by turning them to stone until the fighting was over. But the witch doctor was killed, and the sisters were left trapped in the rock forever!

TRAILBLAZING

Early European settlers believed the Blue Mountains, with their towering cliffs and plunging gullies, were impossible to cross. In 1813, three men were able to prove them wrong. They took three servants, four packhorses, and five dogs with them. They fell sick, lacked food, feared attacks from local Aboriginal people, and the route was backbreaking, but they finally spotted grassland in the distance – which they desperately needed to raise their cattle.

LET THE TRAIN TAKE THE STRAIN

ONE WAY TO GET TO THE BOTTOM OF THE MOUNTAINS IS VIA THE SCENIC RAILWAY – THE STEEPEST PASSENGER TRAIN IN THE WORLD. IT TRAVELS AT AN INCLINE OF 52 DEGREES, BUT PASSENGERS CAN MAKE THIS FEEL EVEN STEEPER BY TILTING THEIR ADJUSTABLE SEATS. A SEE-THROUGH GLASS ROOF MAKES SURE THEY CAN STILL TAKE IN THE VIEW.

FLOAT ON...

Yachts, ferries, super-cruisers, and beach floats, there's no end to the ways people use the harbor waters. There are watery museums in Sydney, too, and even Water Police to keep everything under control.

A GLASS BOTTOM
SYDNEY SEA LIFE AQUARIUM

Visitors have a predator's-eye view of tropical fish, sawfish, and sharks, as well as getting a peek behind the scenes on this trip inside the aquarium, on a boat with a glass bottom! Not so like a predator, they get to feed the fish in the barrier reef tank and at certain times of day those fish include four types of hungry shark. Yikes

WHALE OF A RIDE
MANLY FERRY

Ferries have been sailing around Sydney since 1789, and in 1861, a regular service started from the North Shore across the harbor. Today, the journey from Manly only takes half an hour, but the views are some of the best in the city, especially in June or July, when passengers on their way to work could find themselves waving to some passing whales.

A FERRYTHON TAKES PLACE IN THE HARBOR ON AUSTRALIA DAY (JANUARY 26) EACH YEAR. FOUR FERRIES, ALL DRESSED UP WITH FLAGS AND BANNERS, ARE PACKED WITH PASSENGERS WHO HAVE TO WIN A LOTTERY TO GET A RIDE. THE FIRST FERRY PAST THE HARBOUR BRIDGE WINS THE RACE, BUT NOT NECESSARILY THE BEST-DRESSED BOAT PRIZE!

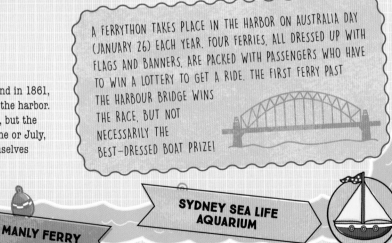

START

MANLY FERRY

SYDNEY SEA LIFE AQUARIUM

CRUISING AROUND

SYDNEY HARBOUR

Sydney is Oz's most popular destination for cruise ships, and these floating hotels look vast, even against the backdrop of Sydney Harbour Bridge. The mammoth Voyager-class cruiser is truly state of the art. Cabins without sea views have virtual balconies on long screens, so passengers still get a real-time view of the sea outside. The huge range of activities available includes swimming, ice-skating, rock climbing, shopping, and live shows.

SYDNEY HARBOUR

BEARE PARK

SUNSET SAILING

BEARE PARK

Early on Wednesday and Friday evenings, up to 100 yachts take to the water as they race around the harbor. Not all the crews are experienced. Some are on tourist trips and may be first-time sailors. They're well and truly thrown in at the deep end, but with plenty of help and encouragement, there's a small chance they could win the race.

THE ROLEX SYDNEY HOBART YACHT RACE IS OZ'S MOST FAMOUS, AND PROBABLY THE MOST GRUELING, LONG OCEAN RACE IN THE WORLD. CROWDS LINE THE HARBOR TO WAVE THE BOATS OFF ON THE 3–4 DAY SAIL TO THE ISLAND OF TASMANIA.

FLOATING FUZZ

BALMAIN, SYDNEY HARBOUR

A lot can happen on and under all that harbor water, so the Water Police have an important role to play. Today, they include divers, detectives, crime-prevention officers, and even a marine intelligence unit. Police boats can whip through the water at high speed, patrolling the waters, checking for drunk drivers, and making sure boats carry life jackets.

THE WATER POLICE HAD THEIR BEGINNINGS IN A "ROW BOAT GUARD" SET UP BY GOVERNOR PHILLIP, IN 1789, TO WATCH OUT FOR SMUGGLERS AND STOP CONVICTS SNEAKING LETTERS TO THE CREW OF PASSING SHIPS.

BALMAIN, SYDNEY HARBOUR

AUSTRALIAN NATIONAL MARITIME MUSEUM

PASSENGER PERILS

AUSTRALIAN NATIONAL MARITIME MUSEUM

Every type of vessel is represented in this museum, with a few whole ships on show in the water outside. Inside, exhibitions tell passengers' stories of traveling to Australia. If the conditions were bad for convicts, a 19th-century passenger ship wasn't much better. Those on board commonly suffered from seasickness, diarrhea, and constipation. When the waters got choppy, there were sprains, bruises, and even broken bones. Passengers also had to cope with the heat of the tropics, not to mention any diseases picked up on the way. To cap it all off, sometimes the ship's captain had to be the doctor, too!

FLOAT PARTY
ROSE BAY

The weather on Australia Day, in January, is usually sunny and HOT, so people flock to this beach with any inflatable they can find. There might be blow-up mattresses, beach floats, sofas, swimming pools, and every inflatable animal you can imagine bobbing about in the water. On Bondi Beach, inflatable flip-flops are given out each year in an attempt to smash the Guinness World Record for the longest line of floating flip-flops in the water.

NOT EVERYONE IS A FAN OF FLOAT PARTIES. ONE PARTY WAS CANCELLED AFTER 9,000 PEOPLE THREATENED TO TURN UP! LOCALS ARE NOT IMPRESSED BY THE AMOUNT OF TRASH LEFT BEHIND, AND THEY WORRY THAT IT COULD HARM SEA LIFE.

ROSE BAY

WATSONS BAY

DOGGY-PADDLE
WATSONS BAY

Paddle boarding is particularly popular in Watsons Bay. On Australia Day, there's a whole range of races, including one with a twist: the very popular Every Man and His Dog race. It's a 492 ft. (150 m) sprint, and both dog and owner must stay on the board at all times. There's a treasure hunt, too, in which contestants paddle out and stay on the board while their four-legged friends "hunt" for toys in the water.

OFF TO SEE

THE HMB *ENDEAVOUR*

On a wharf alongside the Australian National Maritime Museum in Darling Harbour is one of the most important boats from Australian history – or one that looks just like it. The replica ship took five years to build, following the original plans. If the *Endeavour*'s not at home, it may be taking a crew of novice sailors out for a few days of training.

THE HMB *ENDEAVOUR*

MAN WITH MISSIONS

The real *Endeavour* was the boat Captain James Cook took command of in 1768. The plan was to sail to Tahiti to observe the transit of Venus across the sun, but a second, secret mission was to find the Great South Land, a continent that people thought lay somewhere between New Zealand and America.

VERY IMPORTANT PLANET

Venus was going to move across the sun on June 3, 1769. Around the world, over 150 observers prepared to record the transit, including the *Endeavour*'s onboard astronomer. By putting their findings together, the observers hoped to calculate the distance from Earth to the sun. This transit was very important, because the next one wasn't due for 105 years!

54

SHIP'S FOREMAST STANDS 109.9 FT. (33.5 M) HIGH.

NO MAN'S LAND

COOK SUCCESSFULLY OBSERVED THE TRANSIT OF VENUS BUT FAILED TO FIND A NEW CONTINENT. HOWEVER, HE DID MAP THE NEW ZEALAND COASTLINE. HE THEN SAILED AROUND TO "NEW HOLLAND," WHERE HE NAVIGATED AND MAPPED THE EAST COAST, CLAIMING IT FOR KING GEORGE III OF BRITAIN, UNDER THE NAME OF NEW SOUTH WALES.

THE *ENDEAVOUR'S* ONBOARD BOTANIST, JOSEPH BANKS, WAS REALLY IMPRESSED BY THE PLANT LIFE ON ONE PART OF THE COAST. IT'S NOW KNOWN AS BOTANY BAY.

ON BOARD WERE: 18 MONTHS' SUPPLIES AND 94 MEN, INCLUDING CAPTAIN COOK. ONLY 56 OF THE CREW MADE IT HOME 2 YEARS, 11 MONTHS LATER. MOST DIED OF DYSENTERY AND MALARIA.

LOST SANDWICH

The *Endeavour* was sold after Cook's first expedition, and its name was changed to the *Lord Sandwich*. In 1778, it helped fend off a French invasion of America, but sank to the bottom of Newport Harbor in Rhode Island. For centuries, no one knew the whereabouts of the ship's remains. Recently, archaeologists found several wrecks lying together on the seabed. They're now trying to figure out which one is the *Sandwich*.

search: ENDEAVOUR

368 TONS
The ship's weight.

109 FT.
(33.3 M)
The length of the ship.

28
The number of sails, which take up a whopping 10,000 sq. ft. (930 sq m) of canvas.

ASIA IN OZ

The Chinese were the first to arrive in Sydney from Asia. Today, 7.5 percent of the city's population was actually born in China and, after English, Mandarin is the city's second language. Other Asian cultures are on the rise, though, and among others, Sydney benefits from Thai, Japanese, and Korean influences.

search: IMMIGRATION FACTS

LANGUAGE TEST

In 1888, new laws restricting immigration to Australia were introduced. The "White Australia Policy" was designed to keep out "undesirables." Anyone hoping to enter Australia had to take a 50-word language test in a European language. If an immigration officer wanted to stop someone from entering the country, he'd choose a language the applicant didn't know!

CALM IN THE CITY

CHINESE GARDEN OF FRIENDSHIP

START

CHINESE GARDEN OF FRIENDSHIP

DRAGON GATES, CHINATOWN

How do you fit mountains, rivers, lakes, and waterfalls into one small city park? Easy — make them all in miniature! The Chinese have been designing gardens for 3,000 years, creating wild landscapes rather than lawns and colorful flower beds. The people of Guangzhou, in southern China, gave this garden to the people of Sydney in 1988. The two cities call themselves "sisters," and the garden is a symbol of friendship.

CROSSING CONTINENTS

DRAGON GATES, CHINATOWN

Stepping through the Dragon Gates is like walking into a different continent: Asian pop sounds, delicious food smells, and the bright storefronts make it clear that this is Chinatown. Chinese people settled in Sydney after the gold rushes, many setting up as market gardeners, selling their vegetables door to door. Friendships soon formed across the communities.

UNDERSTAND VIRTUE AND TRUST

信廉德通

35 FT. (10.7 M) HEIGHT OF SCULPTURE

RICH HISTORY

GOLDEN WATER MOUTH, CHINATOWN

The eucalyptus tree at the Haymarket entrance to Chinatown has been turned into a sculpture. Artist Lin Li was born in China but studied sculpture in Australia. Lin has brought her experiences of the two countries together. Her design uses the ancient Chinese energy-balancing philosophy of feng shui and Australian materials. Dripping water symbolizes wealth and life, while gold is a reminder of the Australian gold rushes that brought Chinese miners to Oz in the 1850s.

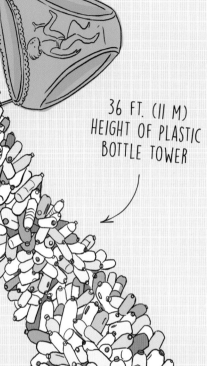

36 FT. (11 M) HEIGHT OF PLASTIC BOTTLE TOWER

GREEN UNDERWEAR AND EMPTY BOTTLES

WHITE RABBIT GALLERY

Chinese artist Wang Zhiyuan prefers to make art from things that are useless. His pieces in this gallery include a huge tower of used plastic bottles, called *Thrown to the Wind*, and a giant pair of decorated green underwear cast from bronze. The gallery owner was so impressed by the originality of Wang Zhiyuan's work that she took a trip to China to find other artists. Only Chinese art is shown in this gallery, and only if it was made after 2000.

WHITE RABBIT GALLERY

GOLDEN WATER MOUTH

THAI TOWN
PITT STREET

In 1901, only 37 Thai people lived in the whole of Australia. The Thai population swelled in the 1970s, and the first Thai restaurant opened in Sydney in 1976 – by 1999, there were over 400! Locals have been calling the end of Pitt Street "Thai Town" for years. It's where they come to find all things Thai. In 2013, three new street signs made the name official. Now Sydney's Thai Town is one of only two in the world outside Thailand.

THE THAI FOOD FESTIVAL GETS BIGGER EVERY YEAR. EVENTS INCLUDE COOKING DEMOS BY SOME OF SYDNEY'S BEST THAI CHEFS, MUSIC FROM THAI POP BANDS, KICK-BOXING DISPLAYS, AND... FINGERNAIL DANCING! DANCERS DON'T NEED REALLY LONG NAILS TO TAKE PART. THEY WEAR FAKE ONES MADE OF BRASS!

PITT STREET

NAN TIEN TEMPLE

PEACE AT LAST
NAN TIEN TEMPLE

The largest Buddhist temple in the southern hemisphere lies 50 miles (80 km) south of Sydney. Its striking eight-story pagoda (tiered tower) is designed to hold 7,000 dead bodies – after they've been cremated. Cremation is reserved for Buddhist followers and their families, but the temple is open to everyone. Visitors can find peace in the Great Hero Hall, in front of five tall Buddhas (and 10,000 tiny ones!). Those who don't know how to meditate can learn here – or take classes in t'ai chi, calligraphy, and origami (paper folding).

MANGA AND MORE

KINOKUNIYA

Cool kids love to hang out at Sydney's biggest bookshop, which has an excellent selection of Manga and graphic novels. It also stocks books in English, French, Chinese, Japanese, and German! The first Kinokuniya shop opened in Tokyo in 1927, and today it's Japan's largest bookstore chain, with 80 shops worldwide. Stores abroad give Japanese people easy access to their home culture and also introduce the culture to new communities.

How many books the store stocks. **300,000**

30% of the books are printed in Chinese and Japanese.

KINOKUNIYA

TOFU OR NOT TOFU?

BODHI RESTAURANT, COOK AND PHILLIP PARK

This Buddhist restaurant only serves Asian vegetarian food, but in among the sweet potato patties and vegetable spring rolls are familiar items such as Peking "Duck," Sweet and Sour "Chicken," and Vegetarian "Prawns"! They're actually serving meat substitutes made from tofu, but they aim to fool even the most dedicated meat-eater.

BODHI RESTAURANT, COOK AND PHILLIP PARK

WALK ON THE WILD SIDE

Australia has some interesting wildlife that's found only in this part of the world. In Sydney, curious creatures can lurk in the water and hang out in zoos, parks, and even back gardens.

START

THE ENTRANCE

WAITING FOR WHALES
BARRENJOEY LIGHTHOUSE

Around 20,000 whales will swim past Sydney between June and November as they migrate north for the winter. The Barrenjoey Lighthouse is the ideal location to spot them from. Whales were once hunted along this coast for their blubber, which was then melted for oil, candles, soap, and perfume. Now, whale tourism brings in much more money.

3,100 MILES
(5,000 KM)
Distance the migrating whales will travel.

"Can someo[ne] put the light down here?"

BARRENJOEY LIGHTHOUSE

PELICAN TEA
THE ENTRANCE

The staff at a fish and chip shop in this vacation town outside Sydney started feeding scraps to the local pelicans years ago. Soon, the birds began to come and ask for their supper. In 1996, the Pelican Plaza feeding platform was built. Now, it's feeding time here at 3:30 p.m., 365 days of the year. This isn't just about free fish. Sometimes, the birds swallow fishhooks or get tangled in fishing line, so at feeding time volunteers can help them out. Today, The Entrance proudly bears the title of "Pelican Capital of Australia."

15.5–19.5 IN.
(40–50 CM)
Length of an Australian pelican's beak.

27 PINTS

The capacity of a pelican's pouch. It's great for catching food in the water, and sometimes it uses its pouch to collect rainwater!

BUSH TALES

NUTCOTE, NEUTRAL BAY

Nutcote was the home of May Gibb, one of Australia's best-loved children's authors and illustrators, for 44 years. She published *Tales of Snugglepot and Cuddlepie* in 1918, and it's never been out of print since. Inspired by the Australian bush, May's main characters are two tiny babies who fit into the shells of the gum nut on a eucalyptus tree. The villains of the piece, the Bad Banksia Men, are creepy-looking cones from the banksia bush, with legs, arms, and faces. Ugh!

Snugglepot and Cuddlepie
Australia 33c

WHALE-WATCHERS WAIT PATIENTLY FOR SIGNS OF:

➡ SPOUTING – BLOWING OUT WATER.

➡ BREACHING – WHOLE WHALE RISING OUT OF THE WATER.

➡ LOBTAILING – TAIL FIN SLAPPING THE WATER.

AND, THANKS TO A SPECIAL WHALE-WATCHING APP, WHATEVER PEOPLE SPOT, THEY CAN SHARE.

NUTCOTE

LANE COVE NATIONAL PARK

MICE UP HIGH

LANE COVE NATIONAL PARK

If you hear rustling overhead in this park, it could mean there are brown antechinus nesting in the trees. These cute creatures are also called marsupial mice, though they aren't really mice at all. They have some unusual habits... antechinuses mate at the same time, then at 11.5 months old, all the males drop dead! Seventy percent of females give birth on the same day, and antechinus moms sometimes have ten babies at once. They give birth at just the right time for the newborns to feast on a sudden glut of insects, such as spiders and cockroaches. Yum!

2.8–5.5 IN. (7–14 CM)
Length of an antechinus.

♀ UP TO 2.5 OZ (71 G)
How much it weighs.

THEY MAY BE MARSUPIALS, BUT ANTECHINUS MOMS DON'T HAVE A POUCH TO CARRY THEIR NEWBORNS IN. INSTEAD, THE BABIES CLING ON TO ONE OF HER TEATS FOR THE FIRST FIVE WEEKS OF THEIR LIVES.

20 YEARS
The longest a blue-tongued lizard has survived in captivity.

TERRIFYING TONGUE
WILD LIFE SYDNEY ZOO

On summer mornings, Sydneysiders may wake up to find a blue-tongued lizard basking in a sunny spot in their garden. Blue-tongues can set up home in old pipes, or a space under the house, living on a diet of tasty slugs and snails. Sydney Zoo specializes in native animals, so here the lizards live side by side with wallabies and wombats. Being a people-friendly creature, it doesn't mind a gentle stroke, but if it wants to chase off a predator, it'll open its large mouth wide and stick out that scary blue tongue.

WILD LIFE SYDNEY ZOO

HYDE PARK

LIVING IN THE CITY
HYDE PARK

Forget zoos with animals kept in enclosures: here, brushtail possums live in the wild, right in the heart of Sydney. Nesting in the branches of fig and eucalyptus trees, they wake up and venture down in the early evening to forage for leftovers, or take a chunk of banana from the hand of a friendly local.

search: POSSUM

○ DEVELOPMENT
A possum baby (joey) develops in its mom's pouch over the winter. It emerges in spring and spends the next couple of months hitching a ride on its mom's back.

○ COMMUNICATION
Both male (jack) and female (jill) possums communicate with one another by making smacking noises. Joeys hiss and sneeze when they feel threatened.

WHEN RAINBOW LORIKEETS STARTED DYING IN LARGE NUMBERS, AUTOPSIES FOUND THAT GRUBBY GARDEN CONTAINERS FILLED WITH SUGARY FOODS WERE TO BLAME. THE BIRDS WERE MALNOURISHED AND DYING OF DISEASES PICKED UP FROM THE CONTAINERS.

PET POTENTIAL

SURRY HILLS

Four-legged friends and their humans are welcome at the Super Furry Festival, which happens in October each year. Visitors can take a picnic with their pooch, visit the kitty cuddle or bunny snuggle tents, or book their dogs in for a "doga" (yoga with your dog!) session. The festival aims to bring animal lovers from far and wide together, and to find homes for animals in need of adoption.

SUPER FURRY FESTIVAL 2016 FEATURED A SPECIAL TREASURE HUNT. DOGS AND OWNERS SEARCHED TOGETHER FOR HIDDEN PRIZES AND TREATS.

BREAKFAST TWEETS

WATSONS BAY

One of Sydney's most common birds is also its most colorful – it looks as though it's had a bath in a paint palette! The rainbow lorikeet likes to eat nectar, fruits, seeds, and insects, and absolutely loves pollen. A special little brush on the end of its tongue helps the lorikeet lick up its food. Sydneysiders with banksia bushes and bottlebrush plants in their gardens could find a flock of these hungry birds turning up for an early-morning breakfast party.

"Don't tell anyone where we hid the honey."

WATSONS BAY

THE WILD ONES

TARONGA ZOO

In 1884, a small zoo was established in a place called Billy Goat Swamp. By 1916, the zoo was too big for the swamp, and 228 mammals, 552 birds, and 64 reptiles had to be ferried by barge to their new home at Taronga! Today, the zoo specializes in wildlife conservation, and its slogan, "For the Wild," reflects the hope that humans and animals can live happily together.

TARONGA ZOO

"Wow, I love the view!"

BIG FRIENDLY DRAGON

Tuka the Komodo dragon died in 2015, aged 33. He'd lived at Taronga Zoo for 24 years and was Australia's largest and most famous lizard. Of course, the Komodo isn't the sort of dragon you find in fairy tales. Nevertheless, it can survive inside the crater of a steaming volcano, it has a forked tongue, and, though it can't fly, it can swim from one Indonesian island to another. Tuka definitely wasn't a monster; he liked nothing better than having his back scratched by a kind keeper.

6 MILES (10 KM)

Distance from which Komodos can sniff out a meal of a rotting carcass, if the wind blows in the right direction.

3,000

Estimated number of Komodo dragons remaining in the wild.

ANIMAL HOSPITAL

THE ZOO HAS ITS OWN HOSPITAL, WHICH KEEPS ITS RESIDENTS IN TIP-TOP CONDITION. IT ALSO TREATS CREATURES BROUGHT IN FROM THE WILD. PATIENTS IN NEED OF HELP HAVE INCLUDED:

- a green turtle with a fishhook stuck in its throat. After a two-hour operation and a stay at the zoo until it could eat again, it was released back into the wild.

- a greater glider that flew into a barbed-wire fence and was too sick to be released. It now lives at the zoo.

- about 30 little penguins each year, which arrive in the hospital either sick or injured.

4,000+
The number of animals at Taronga Zoo today.

search: ZOO ANIMAL FACTS

📍 KOMODO DRAGON
Scientists only discovered that the Komodo dragon's bite was poisonous in 2005!

📍 GREAT GLIDER
A small marsupial that can fly, or rather glide, from tree to tree with the help of skin flaps that stretch from its elbows to its ankles!

📍 SEA LION
The Australian sea lion is the rarest type of seal in the world.

DEVIL BABIES

A few female and male Tasmanian devils are kept at the zoo for breeding purposes. The world's largest marsupial, Tasmanian devils only exist in the wild on the island of Tasmania. Sadly, a deadly disease, caused when the devils bite each other, is killing off the species. This furry creature was named "devil" by early settlers because of its eerie scream, pink mouth, and large teeth, but it isn't really a killer. It only eats dead animals, helping to tidy up the bush.

LOOKING GOOD

Art, sculpture, dance, fashion — there's loads of good-looking stuff going on around Sydney. Follow this trail through the city and you may not believe your eyes.

FIRE HYDRANT

ESCAPE

START

BONDI TO TAMARAMA

SCULPTURE BY THE SEA
BONDI TO TAMARAMA COASTAL WALK

Walking along this path one day, David Handley noticed natural plinths that he thought would be great for showing off sculptures. That was the spark that started the 1.2-mile (2-km) long outdoor art exhibition that had its 20th birthday in 2016. It's now the largest sculpture exhibition in the world! With a top-notch backdrop of sea and sky, the exhibits can be beautiful, bizarre, wacky, or weird, but they definitely make people think.

THE SCULPTURE BY THE SEA EXHIBITION LASTS FOR 18 DAYS. THE VERY FIRST DISPLAY, IN 1997, LASTED FOR JUST ONE DAY.

PICTURING HISTORY
FOLEY STREET

Centuries ago, there was no cultural buzz in this district – it was no more than a bush track connecting Sydney Harbour to Botany Bay. This street was named after Larry Foley, a bare-knuckle boxer in the 1870s. It's witnessed a whole host of street parades, from the settlers' centenary in 1888 to the Mardi Gras that still runs today. These events are displayed in the massive street art mural, *We Are Here*, which stretches across Foley Street's walls.

FOLEY STREET

MERMAID IN THE MOVIES

POWERHOUSE MUSEUM

Inside this museum is a beautiful old cinema – all that remains of Sydney's classic 1930s cinemas. Visitors can watch old movies, including the lavish 1950s *Million Dollar Mermaid*, about Sydney-born swimmer Annette Kellerman. In 1905, she held all of the women's swimming records, aged just 18! After proving herself as a marathon swimmer and the world's highest female diver, she went on to perform in underwater shows and act in silent movies.

ANNETTE KELLERMAN WAS ALSO A FASHION ICON. SHE DESIGNED THE FIRST WOMEN'S ONE-PIECE BATHING SUIT IN 1905! HER SPECTACULAR WARDROBE IS DISPLAYED AT THE POWERHOUSE MUSEUM.

49 FT. (15 M)

Height of the *We Are Here* mural.

243 FT. (74 M)

How far the mural stretches.

THE SOCIAL OUTFIT

POWERHOUSE MUSEUM

FASHION WITH A CONSCIENCE

THE SOCIAL OUTFIT

The Social Outfit designs, makes, and sells ethically produced clothing, accessories, and goods for the home all under one roof. Its main aim is to train and employ refugees and immigrants, while also encouraging talents they already have. Fabrics used are leftovers from other fashion houses – which means they don't end up in a landfill. The shop sells some completely unique fashions, and profits go back into the enterprise.

PARKING LOT ART

ALASKA PROJECTS, DARLINGHURST

It's difficult for new artists to be able to afford spaces to show their work, so Alaska Projects exhibits work for free in unused spaces. They started out with an old office and a couple of underground parking lots. Exhibitions have since spread to stairwells, elevators, and other unused buildings. Finding the exhibition is all part of the visitor's experience, while the artists can use the space however they like.

ALASKA PROJECTS' EXHIBITION KA, BY SIMON DEL FAVERO, IS A DISPLAY OF SPOOKY-LOOKING MANNEQUIN IMAGES. IT SHOWS THEM IN AN IMAGINARY WORLD WHERE MACHINES HAVE TAKEN OVER FROM HUMANS. CREEPY!

DIAMOND BRIGHT

TAYLOR SQUARE

This is not just a pretty façade; the bright diamond patterns painted on the walls of this old bank building copy the traditional markings of the Kamilaroi people. This is street art by Reko Rennie, who uses his works to explore his aboriginal roots. The words "Always was, always will be," written across the diamond stripes, mean whatever has happened to the land, it will always belong to his people.

TAYLOR SQUARE

STAR DANCERS
SYDNEY DANCE COMPANY

Australia's TV drama *Dance Academy* was filmed here, with the city providing a stunning backdrop for the action and the dance moves. The series told the story of a group of dancing wannabes dreaming of hitting the big time. And in real life, many of the cast did just that, because the show became a massive worldwide hit. Now there's a movie, *Dance Academy: The Comeback*, and many of the stars of the show are quickly making names for themselves in Hollywood.

160+ countries aired the three series of *Dance Academy*.

SYDNEY DANCE COMPANY

LAVENDER BAY

WENDY'S SECRET
LAVENDER BAY

As a girl, Wendy Whitely loved reading *The Secret Garden*, by Frances Hodgson Burnett, but never dreamed she'd ever have one herself. However, years later, to cope with the grief of losing her husband, Wendy began to dig in a disused railroad yard near her house. Gradually, over 20 years and with no experience, she turned it into a fabulous garden. There are no signs to help visitors find it, but it's marked clearly on Google Maps as "Wendy Whiteley's Secret Garden."

SPORTY CITY

Sydneysiders are into all sorts of fun sports, from football and cricket to surfing and skateboarding. You'll discover some unusual activities along this trail, too — involving dogs, snorkels, and axes!

SERIOUS FUN
MANLY BEACH

Surf Life Savers are volunteers who patrol the beaches at weekends. There's been a Surf Life Saving Club here for over 100 years, and to ensure members keep up their fitness and skills, the club organizes carnivals. Crowds come to watch rescue-board racing, surf-boat rowing, and surf swimming, as well as a chariot race and... er... a pillow fight on the beach.

MANLY BEACH

START

DOG DAY

SCOTLAND ISLAND TO CHURCH POINT

SCOTLAND ISLAND TO CHURCH POINT, PITTWATER

According to legend, the Scotland Island Dog Race first happened in 1973, after two ferry captains had an argument over whose dog was faster. They set their dogs to swim the 1,640–1,968 ft. (500–600 m) from Scotland Island to the mainland, and there's been a dog race here on Christmas Eve ever since. Owners pay an entrance fee of a can of beer and a can of dog food, then paddle or swim alongside, shouting encouragement as their dogs whip through the water. The prize for the fastest dog is cans of beer and dog food!

48,000
How many spectators the cricket ground can hold.

THE BLOODS
SYDNEY SWANS

Australian football is a lively game of four quarters, with 18 players a side. The main aim is to get the ball between the two tall goalposts — highest score wins. Players can propel the ball however they like, but they can't throw or run with it. The game started as a way of keeping cricketers fit in the winter months (Sydney Swans, known to fans as "The Bloods," still play on the Sydney Cricket Ground field). Games had no time limit during the 19th century – players carried on until one side scored two goals, the ball burst, or an argument stopped play!

search: AUSTRALIAN FOOTBALL

25 MINUTES
How long each of the game's four quarters lasts.

6
The number of points earned from each goal.

12 HOURS
The longest game ever played. It continued over three Saturdays in 1858 until it was eventually declared a draw!

SYDNEY SWANS

MOORE PARK

"YABBA" (STEPHEN GASCOIGNE) WAS ONE OF AUSTRALIAN CRICKET'S MOST LOYAL FANS. HE MADE A NAME FOR HIMSELF WITH HIS WITTY COMMENTS FROM THE STAND, AND WENT FROM SELLING RABBITS TO WRITING HIS OWN COLUMN IN A SUNDAY NEWSPAPER.

NOW THIS IS CRICKET
SYDNEY CRICKET AND SPORTS GROUND, MOORE PARK

Though cricket is the favorite summer sport for most Sydneysiders, this stadium also accommodates Aussie football, rugby, soccer, baseball, and has even hosted bands, such as the Rolling Stones. As a cricket ground, though, it's one of the world's most famous. Sculptures of four top Aussie cricketers stand on the members' lawn. These include previous captain Steve Waugh, who won a record-breaking 41 out of 57 test matches, and Fred Spofforth, who played from 1877–1887 and was nicknamed "The Demon" for his fast bowling.

RUN TO THE SUN

SYDNEY CITY CENTER TO BONDI BEACH

City2Surf is the largest running event in the world. It begins with wheelchair athletes, who hope to complete the course in around 35 minutes. Next come the fastest runners, aiming for 40–50 minutes. As they finish, the "back of the pack" hasn't even started. These racers are here to have fun – people have dressed up as Smurfs, astronauts, gorillas, and bananas – and many have never run the distance before. Fueled by free candy, drinks, and the party atmosphere, it's amazing how far they can go!

8.7 MILES (14 KM)
The total distance of the City2Surf race.

2,000
The number of runners in 1971.

OVER 80,000
The number of runners in 2016.

CITY CENTER

BONDI BEACH

BOWL-A-RAMA

BONDI BEACH

Bowl-a-Rama takes place each year in what looks like an empty swimming pool. It's actually Oz's biggest skateboarding competition, and the only international pro-skate event that's based around a bowl. Pro-skaters come from around the world, with contests for young and old. Veteran skater Tony Hawk (left) turned up in 2016 and won the Masters (for older skaters). The Girls' Jam has fewer contestants but is getting more popular every year.

7,000
The size of the crowd.

POPPY STARR OLSEN STARTED SKATING AT AGE 8 AND WON HER FIRST CONTEST AT 9. IN 2016, SHE WON THE WORLD SKATEBOARDING TITLE FOR OVER-15 GIRLS

CHOPPING SPREE

SYDNEY SHOWGROUND

Woodchoppers gather at the Sydney Royal Easter Show for the contest of the year. Splinters fly as international axmen and axwomen try to chop down a full-length tree trunk. Anyone can take part: teenage girls, whole families, senior citizens – as long as they know what they're doing. In 2016, a one-armed axman entered. He didn't win, but he definitely didn't come last.

SYDNEY SHOWGROUND

OLYMPIC POOL

UNDERWATER HOCKEY

OLYMPIC POOL, RYDE AQUATIC LEISURE CENTRE

Underwater hockey has been around since the 1950s, but it's just taking off in Sydney. The rules are simple: two teams of six start at opposite ends of the pool. Wearing masks, snorkels, fins, and carrying a stick, they race underwater to reach the weighted puck (disk) in the middle. Each team uses their sticks to try to push the puck to their goal at one end of the pool. Sounds simple, but it's fast-paced and it's happening underwater. While players scramble around at the bottom of the pool, they also have to hold their breath!

GAMES OF 2000

THE SYDNEY OLYMPICS

Sydney hosted the first Olympic Games of the 21st century in 2000, and the president of the International Olympic Committee, no less, declared them "the best Olympic Games ever"! Australia had only hosted the games once before, in Melbourne, 44 years earlier.

47,967 volunteers joined the "Games Force" that set up and helped run the Olympics.

3.6 BILLION people watching at home from around the world.

12,687 The number of performers in the opening ceremony, which included a dance... with lawn mowers!

THE SYDNEY OLYMPICS

SWIM IT TO WIN IT

Rivalry between the US and Aussie swimming teams was building up. Before the games, the US team claimed they'd "smash" the Aussies "like guitars." In the final lap of the 4x100 m relay, both teams were neck and neck, but Ian Thorpe was first to touch the side, winning the race for Australia. His teammates celebrated by strumming air guitars. The US had never lost this race before.

ERIC THE EEL

ERIC "THE EEL" MOUSSAMBANI ENTERED THE 100 M FREESTYLE SWIMMING RACE JUST EIGHT MONTHS AFTER LEARNING TO SWIM. AT HOME IN EQUATORIAL GUINEA, HE HAD NO COACH AND PRACTICED IN A 66 FT. (20 M) POOL. THERE WERE THREE CONTESTANTS IN HIS FIRST HEAT, AND THE OTHER TWO WERE DISQUALIFIED. ERIC SWAM ON ALONE, CHEERED BY 17,000 SPECTATORS, TO A NEW OLYMPIC RECORD — FOR THE SLOWEST 100 M SWIM EVER!

HERE COME THE GIRLS

SYDNEY 2000 CELEBRATED 100 YEARS OF WOMEN COMPETING IN THE OLYMPICS. THE OLYMPIC FLAME ARRIVED AT THE STADIUM IN THE HANDS OF AUSSIE ATHLETE CATHY FREEMAN, WHO ALSO REPRESENTED INDIGENOUS AUSTRALIANS. TEN DAYS LATER, SHE WON GOLD, CHEERED ON BY AN ECSTATIC CROWD, IN THE 400 M FINAL. CATHY THEN PROUDLY RAN A BAREFOOT VICTORY LAP WHILE CARRYING BOTH THE AUSTRALIAN AND THE ABORIGINAL FLAGS.

10,651 ATHLETES FROM **199** COUNTRIES COMPETED IN **300** EVENTS

FREEMAN WINS GOLD IN 49.11 SECONDS.

GREEN GAMES

Back in 2000, the Sydney Olympic stadium was the biggest ever built – holding up to 110,000 spectators. Its clever roof was open in the middle, to keep spectators dry but allow the grass to grow. There was a green theme to the games, so air vents and light shafts were installed to save energy, and rainwater collected from the roof was used to water the field. Even the stadium has been recycled! Reduced in size to seat 83,000, it's due another revamp in 2019.

AU$6.6 BILLION US$4.9 BILLION
The cost of hosting the games.

1,580 ACRES
The size of the Olympic Park.

20 YEARS
The length of time between German kayaker Birgit Fischer's Sydney gold medal and the previous gold she won in Moscow, in 1982. She was the first woman to achieve this in any sport.

FROM ATHENS TO SYDNEY, THE OLYMPIC TORCH TRAVELED FURTHER THAN EVER BEFORE. IT SET OFF ON MAY 10, 2000, AND ARRIVED AT THE SYDNEY OLYMPIC STADIUM ON SEPTEMBER 15.

MUNCH TIME!

Eating out in Sydney can be a real adventure, taking customers around the world without ever leaving their restaurant table. Menus are as varied as the city's population, and sometimes two food traditions collide to create exciting new "fusion foods." From posh nosh to cheap eats, this trail is just a taster.

KING OF TARTS
GEORGE STREET

Adriano Zumbo, king of tarts and all sweet treats, trained in Paris and became a master of the melting French macaron. In his Sydney shops, he sells his very own zumbarons, which normally come in a phenomenal 40 flavors. To celebrate his birthday one year, he increased the range to 60 flavors for one day only. The choices included: strawberry bubblegum, burnt toast and butter, cheeseburger, fried chicken, and Thai green curry!

TASTY PASTRY

PASTIZZI CAFÉ, NEWTOWN

A pastizzi is a filled filo pastry parcel that comes from Malta. This delicious, cheap snack has been a favorite fast food in Malta for centuries, and is traditionally stuffed with cheese and peas. Pastizzi Café has taken the crunchy, flaky treat a step further and offers a choice of tempting fillings, including bacon and egg, chilli con carne, berry and custard, and chocolate and ricotta cheese. If you can't decide which one to have, you can always take some home to put in the freezer.

START

AU$4
(US$3)
The cost of a gourmet pastizzi.

PASTIZZI CAFÉ

ADRIANO NOW HAS HIS OWN TV SHOW, CALLED *JUST DESSERTS*, IN WHICH HE CHALLENGES AMATEUR CHEFS TO COME UP WITH DARING DESSERTS. NO ONE COULD TOP HIS CHOCOLATE WILLY WONKA HAT THAT FLOATS IN THIN AIR!

GEORGE STREET

KEEP IT LOCAL

ALL AROUND TOWN

Settlers didn't take much notice of what Aboriginal people ate when they first arrived, preferring to import their own plants and animals. But bush tucker (food native to Australia) is becoming popular among Australian chefs who are using it to create some dazzling new dishes. How about kangaroo with purple carrot and riberry fruit, caramelized wallaby tail, or wattleseed pancakes?

WATTLESEEDS COME FROM THE ACACIA PLANT AND CAN BE USED TO MAKE FLOUR OR A COFFEE-LIKE DRINK. THE SEEDS ARE REALLY NUTRITIOUS AND THE OUTER HUSKS TREMENDOUSLY TOUGH — THEY CAN SURVIVE FOR 20 YEARS ON THE GROUND, AND MIGHT ONLY GERMINATE AFTER A BUSHFIRE!

ALL AROUND TOWN

QUAY, THE ROCKS

SNOW SURPRISE

QUAY, THE ROCKS

Quay is one of the world's 50 best restaurants, so of course the menu has to be seriously special. You wouldn't eat a "Snow Egg" with toast; it's actually a dessert served in a glass bowl, on a bed of fruit, custard, and icy granita, with the "egg" nestling in the middle. Under a layer of sugary snow, the "shell" of the egg is a cookie (that's been blow-torched into position), while the "white" is perfect poached meringue, which cracks open to reveal a "yolk" oozing delicious fruit ice cream. Wow!

LAMINGTONS — SQUARES OF VANILLA SPONGE CAKE COATED IN CHOCOLATE AND COCONUT — ARE OZ'S MOST FAMOUS CAKES. THEY'RE SOLD IN BAKERIES ALL OVER TOWN.

VANTASTIC

ALL AROUND TOWN

Food trucks can appear anywhere around town, moving locations from one day to the next. One popular street food snack is a Vietnamese pork roll (*Bánh mì thit*). It's a sandwich with a twist – a crispy French-style baguette on the outside and a choice of Asian fillings, pickles, and sauces within. Mama Linh's truck serves pulled pork that's roasted for 12 hours, or crispy chicken with a 25-year-old secret spice recipe.

WOOLLOOMOOLOO

TIGER PIE

HARRY'S CAFÉ DE WHEELS, WOOLLOOMOOLOO

This caravan café has been around for 70 years! Opening in the 1930s, it served pie 'n' peas and crumbled sausages for the dockyard workers. Over the years, its fame has spread, and celebrity visitors include actor Russell Crowe and singer Elton John, who was famously photographed eating a "Tiger." A "Tiger" is any pie of your choice, topped with mashed potatoes, mushy peas, and gravy.

THE "TIGER" PIE IS NAMED AFTER HARRY "TIGER" EDWARDS, WHO FIRST SOLD PIES FROM HIS "CAFÉ DE WHEELS" HERE IN 1938. THE SAME VAN WAS USED FOR OVER 40 YEARS, EVEN THOUGH IT DIDN'T ALWAYS HAVE WHEELS.

FESTIVE FISH

SYDNEY FISH MARKET

Visiting a fish market may not sound too exciting, but this is the largest of its kind in the southern hemisphere, and it's busy, smelly, and fun. The best time to call is before Christmas, when it opens for a full 36 hours, from 5.00am the day before Christmas Eve to 5.00pm on Christmas Eve. Around 110,000 people are likely to shop at any time of the day or night to buy their Christmas fish!

search: FISH MARKET

📍 **728 TONS**
The amount of seafood sold in the 36-hour Christmas opening period.

📍 **2,700**
The number of crates of fish auctioned each day – from 5:30 a.m.

📍 **100+**
The number of fish species for sale here.

SYDNEY FISH MARKET

ALL AROUND TOWN

TOASTIE TO GO

ALL AROUND TOWN

The Jafe Jaffles food truck serves mainly toasted sandwiches, with a wild choice of fillings and some wicked names to match. There's the Jean Claude van Ham – cheese, tomato, and ham; or a David JaffleHoff stuffed with spaghetti Bolognese!

THE JAFFLE (TOASTED SANDWICH) GETS ITS NAME FROM THE MACHINE THAT ONCE MADE IT. THE JAFFLE IRON WAS PATENTED IN 1949 BY DR. ERNEST E. SMITHERS. BY THE 1950S JAFFLE IRONS WERE AN AUSSIE KITCHEN ESSENTIAL.

DEADLY SYDNEY

While newcomers to Oz may worry about killer spiders, snakes, and sharks, Sydney's early immigrants also faced many other lurking dangers, including violent razor gangs and dreadful diseases.

100
sea rescues occur each week in peak season at Tamarama Beach.

Wherever there's a beach patrol, always swim between the red and yellow flags.

START

BEWARE OF THE WATER
TAMARAMA BEACH

It's one of Sydney's most beautiful beaches – and one of Australia's most dangerous. When the water looks perfect for surfing, with plenty of breaking waves, it's actually at its most treacherous. As waves break on the shore, a lot of that water travels back out to sea in rip currents. Rips are where the sea looks calm, but they're actually deep, dark, and fast-moving channels of water. A rip can drag even the strongest of swimmers out to sea scarily fast.

TAMARAMA BEACH

SUN SAFETY
ALL AROUND TOWN

ALL AROUND TOWN

The sun's ultraviolet (UV) rays are dangerous, too – sunburn can be a killer. Sydney weather forecasts include an index to show how strong the UV rays are at different times of day, so people know when sun protection is needed. Australian schoolchildren learn to stay in the shade, wear sunhats, sunglasses, and clothes that cover their skin, and to apply good-quality, high-SPF sunscreen.

FEAR OF THE FUNNEL-WEB

NORTH SHORE

While female funnel-web spiders hide in their burrows at night, hoping an unsuspecting creature will trip on the silk trap she's laid outside her door, the males wander about looking for a mate. That's how they end up trapped in garages, or finding their way inside houses. Only the male contains the deadly chemical that can kill a human. Luckily, an antivenom was developed in 1981, and no one has died from a funnel-web bite since. Phew!

15 MINUTES
How fast a funnel-web bite can kill a person, making it the deadliest spider in the world!

OVER 6.6 FT. (2 M) Length of a full-grown common brown snake.

SNAKEBITE

FEATHERDALE WILDLIFE PARK

There are many kinds of snakes living around Sydney, but you can see them up close at this wildlife park. Snakes don't often bite out in the wild, and if a victim knows they've been bitten, they can be treated. Problems arise when victims don't realize they've been bitten. The common brown snake has such small fangs that its bite might just feel like a scratch.

A DEADLY STOKES' SEA SNAKE WASHED UP ON MANLY BEACH IN 2015, WITH FANGS LONG ENOUGH TO PIERCE A WET SUIT AND VENOM THAT HAS NO ANTIDOTE! IT WAS A FEW THOUSAND MILES FROM ITS USUAL HOME.

IT'S SAID FUNNEL-WEB SPIDERS ARE MOST LIKELY TO BE FOUND ON SYDNEY'S NORTH SHORE, WHERE SOME OF THE POSHEST HOUSES (AND GARDENS) ARE FOUND.

FEATHERDALE WILDLIFE PARK

81

DIRTY RATS

DARLING HARBOUR

The dreaded bubonic plague hit Sydney in 1900, arriving by boat and quickly inflicting its victims with a headache, vomiting, and dizziness, before the lumps appeared. Captain Thomas Dudley, who worked at the harbor, fell ill and was the first to die after pulling dead rats from his toilet! Everyone knew that rats had something to do with the disease, and in the cleanup that followed, locals were paid to hunt them, as well as to disinfect, burn, and demolish buildings – sometimes even their own homes!

A BLOODY BATTLE

DARLINGHURST AND KINGS CROSS

Changes in the law led two women to rise to the top of Sydney's criminal pack. Tilly Devine and Kate Leigh were sworn enemies and guarded their murky empires jealously. In 1927, anyone carrying a gun without a licence could be thrown in prison, and as a result, each woman had a "razor gang" – all members carried deadly cutthroat razors. The two gangs famously clashed in a backstreet, in what is now called the "Battle of Blood Alley."

DARLINGHURST AND KINGS CROSS

RESEARCH BY LOCAL MEDICAL OFFICERS HELPED PEOPLE UNDERSTAND THAT DISEASE COULD BE SPREAD BY INSECTS — IN THIS CASE, THE FLEAS THAT HAD HITCHED A RIDE ON THE RATS' FUR.

SYDNEY'S GRIMY SIDE

JUSTICE AND POLICE MUSEUM

This was once Sydney's Water Police station and magistrate's court. Now, cutthroat razors are on display, along with a whole array of awful weapons. This museum reveals the grimier side of Sydney's past. There's a stuffed dog that helped to solve a murder, an archive of thousands of criminal mug shots, and casts from the teeth of two prisoners that matched a half-eaten chocolate bar left at a crime scene.

THERE'S BEEN A MUSEUM OF CRIME IN SYDNEY SINCE 1910, DISPLAYING EVIDENCE, CRIMINAL TOOLS, AND RECORDS DATING BACK TO THE 1870S. IT WAS USED TO EDUCATE NEW OFFICERS ABOUT THE DEVIOUS WORKINGS OF THE CRIMINAL MIND!

JUSTICE AND POLICE MUSEUM

QUARANTINE STATION

DREADFUL DISEASES

QUARANTINE STATION, MANLY

This lonely peninsula seemed the perfect spot to offload immigrants arriving in Sydney with dreadful diseases. Smallpox, cholera, typhoid, and other deadly conditions mustn't get into the city! In 1877, despite several ships being quarantined in the harbor, smallpox did reach the Rocks area of Sydney. Infected people from the city were sent to the Quarantine Station, and 19-year-old Catherine Holden was the first Sydneysider to die there.

150
The number of people the station could accommodate in 1853.

1,200
How many people the station accommodated at its peak in 1909.

580 ships were diverted here between 1828 and 1984.

13,000
people were quarantined here in total.

SHARK ATTACK!

SYDNEY HARBOUR

Australia holds the record for the most fatal shark attacks in the world, and Sydney Harbour has had its fair share. So, what can Sydneysiders do to keep safe while having fun in the water?

SHARK FACT FILE

Great white sharks like deep ocean waters.

Bull sharks can swim in shallow water and even in fresh water.

Tiger sharks will eat just about anything.

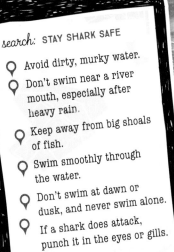

search: STAY SHARK SAFE

- Avoid dirty, murky water.
- Don't swim near a river mouth, especially after heavy rain.
- Keep away from big shoals of fish.
- Swim smoothly through the water.
- Don't swim at dawn or dusk, and never swim alone.
- If a shark does attack, punch it in the eyes or gills.

SYDNEY HARBOUR

SHARK SIGHTED TODAY

ENTER WAT AT OWN RISK

YUCK FACTOR

These large sharks generally think humans taste pretty disgusting. They'd far rather eat a seal, but sometimes they make mistakes. Because they use their mouths to feel, they might swim in for a taste and then swim away once they realize they're not dealing with a seal. Swimmers are much more likely to drown in a rip current (see page 80) than be eaten by a shark.

GREAT WHITE SHARK

SHARK SPY

FIFTY-ONE BEACHES AROUND SYDNEY HARBOUR HAVE SHARK NETS, BUT FROM 1937-2008, 24 OUT OF 38 SHARK ATTACKS HAPPENED ON PROTECTED BEACHES! WHAT'S MORE, THE NETS CAN EVEN KILL SHARKS. TO PROTECT SWIMMERS AND SHARKS, THE GOVERNMENT CONSIDERED HI-TECH ELECTRIC, MAGNETIC, OR EVEN WATER BUBBLE FENCES, BUT IN THE END SETTLED ON LOW-TECH SHARK SPOTTERS — THAT'S PEOPLE WATCHING FROM THE SHORE!

ORDER IN THE OCEAN

Great white sharks only have young every two to three years. It takes 8–12 years for the babies to mature. That's pretty slow for a sea creature, so numbers can dwindle. Great whites maintain order in the ocean by controlling the elephant seal and sea lion populations. That's why the sharks have been protected in Australian waters for over ten years.

STEALTH ATTACK

Paul de Gelder was a navy diver working in the murky waters of Sydney Harbour early one morning when a bull shark attacked him suddenly from below. Paul managed to escape and get back to his boat but was badly injured and lost his hand and leg. Afterwards, he realized he'd missed some shark warning signs that might have stopped him entering the water at all that day.

GOT TO BE GREEN

Like the rest of the world, Sydney is under threat from climate change, with droughts, higher temperatures, and stronger storms. Saving water is a top priority, along with reducing, reusing, and recycling. But it's not all bad news — humans are working hard to find solutions...

40 YEARS!

The 2016 storm was the worst to hit Sydney in four decades.

5.9 IN.
(150 MM)
rainfall in 24 hours.

19 FT.
(6 M)
Height of the waves.

77 MPH
(125 KM/H)
Speed of the winds.

WAVES ON THE WANE

BRONTE BEACH

Experts warn that by the end of the century, climate change will cause a 40 percent drop in the number of huge 11.5 ft. (3.5 m) waves that have made Sydney's seaside a surfer's paradise. Some surfers have already noticed a difference, but for those who prefer to play it safe in the smaller waves, it may not be such a problem.

FEEDING THE BEACH

COLLAROY-NARRABEEN BEACH

This beach is the third most at risk from erosion along the entire Australian coast, and many buildings are dangerously close to the edge. Huge shelves of sand off the Sydney coast might help, though. Scientists say that "beach nourishment" (pumping extra sand onto the beach) can protect against erosion. Tests show that in shifting sand from this shelf, local wildlife wouldn't suffer too much, as this is sand that had washed off local beaches in the first place!

COLLAROY-NARRABEEN BEACH

START

BRONTE
BEACH

KEEPING IT GREEN
THE GROUNDS OF ALEXANDRIA

The Grounds is a green café, bakery, and restaurant – oh, and a mini-farm! Cyclists and drivers who arrive with a full load of passengers win a free coffee for helping to reduce air pollution. The bakery makes its own bread with flour that's hand-milled on the premises. Seasonal crops grown in the organic garden go straight to the kitchen, then to the table. Each day, the on-site composter soaks up everyone's leftovers, which eventually go back onto the garden.

ANIMALS AT THE GROUNDS MINI-FARM INCLUDE: NAUGHTY THE GOAT, MERYL SHEEP, AND THE ROWDY CHICKEN GANG. THEN THERE'S KEVIN BACON (THE PIG), WHO ENJOYS MINGLING WITH VISITORS ON HIS DAILY STROLL AROUND THE BLOCK. FOR A FEW HOURS EACH DAY, VISITORS CAN MEET, FEED, AND PET THE ANIMALS.

NOT THAT SORT OF BANK

AUSTRALIAN PLANTBANK

There are no gold bars in this bank, but what's inside could help save the planet! The mission of the Australian PlantBank is to collect and store seeds from all NSW plants. The seeds are dried, bagged, and frozen at -4°F (-20°C). As only the best will do, each one is X-rayed first, to check it's in tip-top condition, with no insects hiding inside. The seeds last for hundreds of years! So, if a species becomes extinct, the seed bank can replant it.

10,400
The number of seed collections.

50%
of NSW threatened species are stored in the PlantBank.

RECYCLED RUINS

PADDINGTON RESERVOIR GARDENS

Completed in 1866, Paddington Reservoir supplied water to the city for 33 years. After that, the space became a garage, then a gas station, until, in 1990, the roof fell in. In 2009, the remaining structure was turned into a secret sunken garden, right next to the hustle and bustle of Sydney's Oxford Street. Instead of completely rebuilding the space, old arches, pillars, and walls were left standing.

> OVER 2 MILLION GALLONS (9 MILLION LITERS) OF WATER WERE ONCE STORED IN THE UNDERGROUND RESERVOIR TANK. IT'S NOW BEEN RECYCLED INTO A MEGA-PARTY VENUE!

PADDINGTON RESERVOIR GARDENS

FLOATING FOREST

SS AYRFIELD

The SS *Ayrfield* was built over 100 years ago. For most of its life, the ship carried coal, but during World War II, it took supplies to troops. In 1972, it sailed its final voyage, into Homebush Bay, to be taken apart. The hull of the ship still haunts the bay, though. Amazingly, mangrove trees have gradually taken root, turning the rusty wreck into a floating forest and attracting visitors.

SS AYRFIELD

ONE CENTRAL PARK

GREEN WALLS

ONE CENTRAL PARK

Plants grow up its sides, and there is a giant "cooker grill" sticking out of one wall, but this was voted "Best Tall Building Worldwide" in 2014! That's because the green walls are actually vertical gardens. Plant roots are attached by a moist mesh and watered via remote control (using recycled water, of course!). The "cooker grill" is, in fact, a "heliostat" – a device made up of moving mirrored panels. At different times of day, the mirrors redirect sunlight to shadier areas of the park below to save electricity.

"I love the view from my garden!"

search: ONE CENTRAL PARK FACTS

APARTMENTS
The building is home to 623 apartments.

GARDENS
The vertical gardens are 380 ft. (116 m) high and contain 35,200 plants.

HOW GREEN?
The building will save 149,914 tons of greenhouse gas over a 25-year period.

WET, WET, WET

Sydney's watery border is one of the world's most famous sights, but water also features in other ways around the city. This trail includes fountains, dams, and water sculptures, and even rubs noses with a watery pig!

START

WONDERFUL WATERBALL

FITZROY GARDENS

In 1959, Bob Woodward entered a competition to design a fountain – he wasn't expecting to win, but he did! His *El Alamein Memorial Fountain* became a symbol of Sydney and completely changed his career. Bob created a "ball of water" using water spouts supported on a central stalk. When water jets out of each spout, it forms a disc that looks like a dandelion seedpod. The effect caused a sensation, and Bob gave up architecture to continue designing fountains.

211
The number of "stalks" on the dandelion.

18 IN. (45 CM) WIDE
The size of the water "discs" created as the water spouts out of each stalk.

BEARE PARK

FITZROY GARDENS

FANCY FOUNTAINS

BEARE PARK

In the days before you could turn on a faucet to get water at home, fountains – or "bubblers" as Sydneysiders call them – helped cool down the locals, especially when the heat was intense. The mayor ordered eight of these fancy cast-iron drinking fountains to be placed around the city.

NEW SPLASH

ANZAC MEMORIAL, HYDE PARK

Hyde Park holds a magnificent memorial to World War I soldiers. It was completed in 1934 with a stylish memorial building, which is reflected in a calming pool lined by poplar trees. The shape of the pool and the trees are intended to remind people of the River Somme, in France, where Australian troops fought some of their bloodiest battles.

ANZAC MEMORIAL

FUNDS FOR THE MEMORIAL RAN OUT BECAUSE OF THE GREAT DEPRESSION, AND A SECOND WATER FEATURE DESIGNED FOR THE OTHER SIDE OF THE BUILDING WAS NEVER COMPLETED — UNTIL NOW. THE NEW CASCADE FOUNTAIN SHOULD BE FINISHED IN 2018.

A ROCK WITH A VIEW

MRS. MACQUARIE'S CHAIR

Governor Lachlan Macquarie and his wife, Elizabeth, arrived in 1810 on a mission to transform Sydney's image from a grubby convict town to one that the British Empire could be proud of. Elizabeth's favorite view was from this peninsula (now called Mrs. Macquarie's Point), which looked out over the harbor towards the Pacific Ocean. Convicts carved her "chair" out of rock and built a road leading up to it, called – surprise, surprise – Mrs. Macquarie's Road!

ELIZABETH MACQUARIE'S BOOKS ON ARCHITECTURE INSPIRED MANY OF THE NEW BUILDINGS COMMISSIONED IN SYDNEY DURING HER HUSBAND'S 11 YEARS AS GOVERNOR.

MRS. MACQUARIE'S CHAIR

GHOST WALLS

PASSAGE, MARTIN PLACE

The *Passage* water sculpture, built in 2001, marks the spot where houses were demolished in the 1930s to make way for traffic. Black granite outlines where the walls of the houses once stood. Every ten minutes mist rises spookily through gratings in the ground, a ghostly reminder of the long-lost buildings. Three bronze bowl-shaped fountains symbolize the container that would have been used to carry water from the Tank Stream (see page 11) to use in the washrooms and kitchens of the Georgian houses.

ON ESPECIALLY WINDY DAYS THE *PASSAGE'S* MIST HAS TO BE TURNED OFF TO STOP PASSERS-BY GETTING AN UNEXPECTED SOAKING!

PASSAGE

LUCKY LITTLE PIG

MACQUARIE STREET

Il Porcellino means "the little pig" – an interesting name for a statue of a full-sized wild boar! This fountain stands in front of Sydney Hospital, and was donated to raise money in memory of two Italian surgeons who once worked there. It's said if passers-by rub the boar's nose and make a wish, they'll have good luck — as will the hospital, which gets to collect and keep the donations that people toss into the fountain water below.

GOING CONCERN

UNDER SYDNEY HARBOUR BRIDGE

In the 1880s, Sydney city center had a pressing problem. People had nowhere to "go"! As a result, men often went for a pee in the street, but women just had to wait. Cast-iron urinals were erected in busy areas – but were only for men! It wasn't just the public spaces that lacked toilets, many houses had faulty plumbing, or no toilets at all. The local government was finally forced to take action in 1900 – after an outbreak of bubonic plague! Realizing the need for better sanitation, they began to build toilets and sanitary sewage systems underground.

"Wait? That's not fair!"

UNDER SYDNEY HARBOUR BRIDGE

WARRAGAMBA DAM

WHAT A LOTTA WATER

WARRAGAMBA DAM

Containing four times the amount of water held in Sydney Harbour, Warragamba is one of the largest dams in the world, providing fresh water for use in the home. It's built to cope with droughts and withstand floods, but the dam walls had to be raised by 16 ft. (5 m) in the 1980s to allow for new predictions of how high floodwaters could rise.

1,800 people worked around the clock...

3 SHIFTS A DAY 7 DAYS A WEEK

12 YEARS (from 1948–1960) **TO COMPLETE**

COAT HANGER

SYDNEY HARBOUR BRIDGE

It's hard to imagine a time when Sydney Harbour didn't have a bridge. When it opened, in 1932, "the coat hanger," as locals like to call it, was the largest steel arched bridge in the world. Instead of taking a ferry or traveling the 12 miles (20 km) by land to get to the opposite shore, they could now get across the river on foot or by car, train, tram, or horse!

SYDNEY HARBOUR BRIDGE

GOING UP

THE BRIDGE WAS CONSTRUCTED IN SECTIONS THAT WERE TRANSPORTED TO THE SITE, READY FOR WORKERS TO BEAT, WELD, AND RIVET INTO PLACE. THIS WAS THE TIME OF THE GREAT DEPRESSION, AND JOBS WERE HARD TO FIND, SO MOST OF THE 1,400 WORKERS WILLINGLY CLIMBED THE 426.5 FT. (130 M) TO WORK — WITHOUT A HARNESS OR A HARD HAT!

6 MILLION RIVETS WERE USED TO BUILD THE STRUCTURE

THE BRIDGE IS TALLER ON WARMER DAYS BECAUSE THE STEEL EXPANDS WITH THE HEAT. IT CAN ADD UP TO 7 IN. (18 CM) TO THE HEIGHT OF THE ARCH.

GRAND OPENING

Three days before the opening, 52,000 schoolchildren were invited to walk across the bridge as a special celebration. The official opening day was March 19, 1932. Crowds, estimated at 300,000 by some and 1 million by others, watched carnival floats and marching bands parade across the bridge, a procession of ships sail underneath, planes fly overhead, and the first Harbour Bridge fireworks display.

TOWERING MUSEUM

The four granite-covered concrete pylons are 292 ft. (89 m) tall and mainly for show, though there is a museum inside one of them.

BIRD'S—EYE VIEW

The view from the top is probably the most spectacular in the whole of Sydney, and regular tours guide visitors up – wearing harnesses and hard hats. For early birds, setting off in the dark, at 3:00 a.m. in the morning, is the best time to climb. Once they've climbed the 200 steps, they'll be rewarded with a sunrise.

search: BRIDGE MAINTENANCE

⦿ Every day, workers hang from baskets, ridding the bridge of rust, as commuters travel underneath. Nets below the baskets make sure no stray paintbrushes clatter onto the car roofs below.

⦿ Every ten years the road surface has to be replaced.

⦿ Every four to six months new flags replace the old ones.

SYDNEY IN THE DARK

There's lots going on at night in Sydney, and the skyline is spectacular any day of the year. Then, there are the sunsets, the fireworks displays, and the Vivid Sydney light festival, when the views are unbelievable.

"I need a bear hug!"

TARONGA ZOO

START

SYDNEY HARBOUR BRIDGE

ROAR AND SNORE
TARONGA ZOO

After everyone's gone home for the day, a few lucky people — who've bought a Roar & Snore sleepover ticket — are allowed into Taronga Zoo after dark. They get to take a private peek at the animals, and maybe cuddle a koala or feed a giraffe. They eat at the zoo, too, then sleep in comfy tents with a fabulous view of the harbor.

BRIDGE OF LIGHTS
SYDNEY HARBOUR BRIDGE

Sydney authorities claim their city is "New Year's Eve Capital of the World," so a huge amount of effort goes into each New Year's Eve (NYE) fireworks display. One hundred thousand special effects take time to prepare, and 45 pyrotechnicians begin work 16 months earlier. The pressure is on because each midnight display is watched live by 1.6 million people in Sydney alone, and over 1 billion viewers worldwide watch them on TV!

SATURDAY FIREWORKS

DARLING HARBOUR

Sydneysiders don't have to wait until New Year's Eve for fireworks — there are displays at Darling Harbour most Saturday nights. This area has a big industrial history. Early exports of frozen food came from here, with a first shipment of meat to London in 1877. But the industry is long gone and, since 1988, this has been the place to visit for food, fun... and fireworks!

DARLING HARBOUR

80

Around 80 movies from 26 different countries are shown over 17 nights.

search: NYE FIREWORKS

○ **AU$7.2 MILLION**
Total cost of the New Year's Eve display.

○ **12 MINUTES**
How long the display lasts.

○ **7 TONS**
The weight of the fireworks.

○ **37 MILES (60 KM)**
Length of the wires that link the fireworks to computer controls.

○ **130**
The number of firing points on Sydney Harbour Bridge. There are also points on Sydney Opera House and seven barges in the harbor.

NIGHT OWLS

DARLING QUARTER

As the January skies darken, the screens light up for the Night Owls kids' film festival. Every evening during the festival, big name family movies are shown alongside short films from around the world. A panel of children judge and award the best local and international films, as well as those made by children. Anyone can enter a film, as long as they're under 18.

DARLING QUARTER

VIVID SYDNEY

SYDNEY OPERA HOUSE

Each year in June, the Vivid Sydney festival transforms the city center through light. In 2016, its 90 works included:

➡️ a giant heart that asked two people to shout a deafening "I love you" together — the louder they shouted, the brighter the heart glowed.

➡️ the Museum of Contemporary Art, dripping with paint.

➡️ a "cathedral of light" in the Botanical Gardens — this was a 230 ft. (70 m) long tunnel illuminated by tens of thousands of LED bulbs.

➡️ huge dark creatures crawling across the white shell roof of the Sydney Opera House, showing off the work of local indigenous artists in a gigantic moving painting.

SYDNEY OPERA HOUSE

MUSEUM OF CONTEMPORARY ART

KEEP ON LAUGHING

MUSEUM OF CONTEMPORARY ART

Once a week, this museum stays open late to show off the work of some extraordinary artists, such as the Barbara Cleveland Institute, a group of Sydney artists. Their video *One Hour Laugh* shows four women laughing... er... for a whole hour, while wearing colored pointy hats, bibs, and fake eyebrows! Laughing for so long is not as easy as you might think, and the women actually go through a whole range of emotions.

COCKATOO ISLAND

A NIGHT OFFSHORE

COCKATOO ISLAND

Putting its past as a prison, shipyard, and reform school behind it, these days Cockatoo Island is a hip place to be. It's the only Sydney Harbour island where you can stay overnight. There are gigs and a regular arts festival, and anyone who can't face the ferry home can check in to one of the luxury apartments or houses, or crash out in a fully equipped tent at the stunning waterside campsite.

HUGH JACKMAN FILMED PART OF THE MOVIE *X-MEN ORIGINS: WOLVERINE* HERE IN THE DARKNESS OF SOME OF THE OLD BUILDINGS THAT STILL STAND ON COCKATOO ISLAND.

SUNSATIONAL

PARRAMATTA RIVER

Sydney's sunsets are often sensational and there's no better way to view one than from the river. For a few nights in 2016, locals reckoned the sunsets were better than ever. Forecasters suggested it was a mixture of calm weather, high clouds, and the position of the sun. But the fire service claimed the spectacular skies were enhanced by blazes they were lighting to stop the spread of bushfires! They advised people to close their windows and stay indoors.

PARRAMATTA RIVER

INDEX

INDEX

FURTHER READING

The Cities Book
Lonely Planet Kids, 2016

This worldwide travel guide aimed at kids is crammed with really useful information on lots of cities, including Sydney, Melbourne, Ballarat, Perth, and Darwin.

The Magic Pudding
by Norman Lindsay

This wildly funny story follows the adventures of four animal friends and their magic pudding. It's a world-famous Australian children's classic full of amazing characters and witty songs, and so it's definitely worth a read!

This is Australia
by Miroslav Sasek

This quirky book is full of really cool illustrations and information. It is perfect for a school project on Australia, as it contains historical as well as current facts – some serious and some fun.

The Forgotten Pearl
by Belinda Murrell

Aimed at older children, this tells the story of Pearl Harbor from the perspective of a young girl, and paints an interesting picture of Sydney during World Was II.

Captain Cook (Famous Lives)
by Rebecca Levene

Discover Australia with Captain Cook and see what Sydney was like many years ago before the Europeans arrived. This book puts Sydney and Australia in a worldwide context that is easily accessible for younger children.

Stories from the Billabong
by James Vance Marshall

This book tells ten of Australia's ancient aboriginal legends, with amazing illustrations by Aboriginal artist and storyteller Francis Firebrace.